eat * sleep * shop

# PARIS
## STYLE GUIDE

*Elodie Rambaud*

**MURDOCH BOOKS**

# Contents

06     *When to visit?*

08     *Trade shows & festivals*

10     *Communicating & getting around*

12     *A weekend in Paris*

16     *A few hotels ...*

18     *A few restaurants ...*

20     *A few indulgences ...*

22     *A few bars ...*

24     *A few (good) cafés ...*

26     *To market, to market ...*

## 01

### CONTEMPORARY INSPIRATION

Be inspired by this selection of the city's concept stores, trendsetters and newsmakers, creative designers, style alchemists and image-makers. You won't find any shrinking violets here!

30

## 02

### TEXTILES

Paris' fabric designers are highly regarded. Smaller independent stores offer more personalised ranges, crafted by hand using traditional techniques. You'll find a more individual product. Textiles, Paris style.

52

## 03

### NATURE & BOTANICALS

Some things engage us through our senses. That haunting fragrance, the soft brush of a feather, a sumptuous colour, a gritty texture, the solitude of a garden—each evoking a memory. It's only natural.

70

### ART & COLOUR

Meet treasured artisans and discover some of Paris' finest art supplies stores. Who knows, you might even be inspired to explore your own creative talents.

**04**

94

## 05 TOOL BOX

Some places selling tools and equipment have been in the game for many years and are still in all their original, unadulterated glory. Specialist knowledge and quality products are their tools of trade.

*116*

## 06 VINTAGE

Meet antiques dealers who are passionate about art history and store owners with a knack for unearthing the latest must-have object. Plus a guided tour through the Saint-Ouen flea market with its 1700 vendors.

*138*

## 07 WORLD DÉCOR

A single object can transport you thousands of miles away, evoke memories of the essence of a place and take you on a journey around the world. Imagine what a whole shopful could do!

*182*

## 08 TABLE

Scattered across Paris, these smaller tableware and kitchen stores have innovative selections and pieces you won't see everywhere else.

*198*

## 09 ACCESSORIES

An accessory sets the tone and brings the whole together. In these Aladdin's caves you'll discover recent and vintage treasures to help express your personality and originality.

*220*

## 10 CHILDREN

Good shops dedicated to decorating for children aren't so easy to find in Paris, but a few concept stores have established themselves and are now among the most innovative and envied in the world.

*240*

*258* **MAPS & INDEX**

*Whether you are a Parisian native or fresh off the plane after a 15-hour flight, you're probably keen to explore the streets and alleyways of Paris. It was a similar sense of eagerness and curiosity that led me to write this book. Hold on to that enthusiasm, it will lead you to discover some amazing things.*

Fabulous fabrics made from natural fibres, film for your Polaroid camera, Chanel embroideries, a bell jar for a future cabinet of curiosities, a stone sink, an electrical cord covered in woven fabric and black-tinted roses. You can cycle along the riverbank on your vintage bike and have your business cards engraved at a printing house like it's 1912. Extraordinary places and experiences await you.

I live and work in Paris as a prop stylist for media, publishing and advertising. I love thinking about how to assemble objects, colours and textures to create visual stories and identities. My special fields are lifestyle, food and decorating—everything that is done with passion, individuality and elegance. I spend my time exploring the city and the internet in search of that unexpected object, the perfect accessory or ideal colour that will make all the difference to a photo. I check out every new trend and project, always on the lookout for individuals who are creating the style of Paris, providing me with visual, graphic and aesthetic inspiration.

In these pages you'll discover my favourite addresses in Paris, grouped into ten chapters. You may already know some of these places, and others I hope will surprise you, just as they surprised me when I first discovered them. At the end of the book there are maps of the main arrondissements to help you locate these remarkable spots. Nothing will be left to chance, except perhaps the joy of serendipitously stumbling upon some new gem.

Paris. Make the most of it. Wander through its streets and gardens, through its lovely shops, succumb to its pâtisseries, stroll over the Pont des Arts, dream to the sound of a distant accordion on a summer evening. And do it all with style.

Dior

Dior

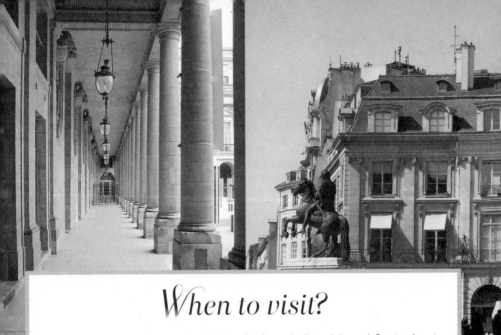

# When to visit?

Spring and autumn are particularly lovely: from April to July and September to November, the weather is generally good. You can check out the Paris weather site METEO-PARIS.COM, which is fairly reliable as weather sites go.

In spring, with the first sunny days, the café terraces come to life, fresh colours overrun the window displays and second-hand markets and 'junk' sales happen around the capital almost every weekend. The collective mood in Paris is rosy. Autumn, meanwhile, is an especially heady season. After two months of summer lull, suntanned Parisians return to the capital. It's the launch of the literary and film seasons, the museums reveal their new exhibitions, the evenings are still mild and long and the shops that closed during August reopen with new colours and fabrics that set the tone for winter. September and January bring the famous **MAISON & OBJET** trade show and its fringe events, which attract tastemakers from all over the world.

The sales generally start from 10 January for the winter collections and around 26 June for summer; each lasts a month.

PATISSERIE

# Trade shows

*If you want to visit Paris and take advantage of the professional trade shows, these are the ones not to be missed.*

The traditional **MAISON & OBJET** trade show opens its doors in September and January. M&O is an intense four-day event detailing new trends in decoration and design. There are representatives from every country. Running concurrently is the Paris Déco Off, a textile fair that takes place throughout showrooms in the capital. MAISON-OBJET.COM / PARIS-DECO-OFF.COM

**FIAC** The *Foire Internationale d'Art Contemporain*—the international contemporary art fair—is held each October at the Grand Palais. FIAC.COM

**LE SALON DU VINTAGE** is held each year in the Marais, where a huge space is given over to vintage objects from furniture to fashion (includes Yves Saint Laurent, Christian Dior ...) SALONDUVINTAGE.COM

**PARIS PHOTO** is the annual international trade show of contemporary and period photography in Paris. It takes place in mid-November at the Grand Palais. PARISPHOTO.COM

**LES JOURNÉES DE LA CÉRAMIQUE** happens every year on Place Saint-Sulpice and turns the spotlight on ceramic art and design. There are wonderful discoveries to be made there and you can also buy pieces. It's best to have some cash on hand, as credit cards are generally not accepted. LESJOURNEESDELACERAMIQUEPARIS.FR

**LE SALON ANTIQUITÉ BROCANTE DE LA BASTILLE** is an unmissable trade show in the heart of Paris, with 70 antique dealers and nearly 300 dealers of second-hand goods. Although it can be a little expensive, it's in the perfect location above the Port de l'Arsenal, a pleasant place to stroll around in springtime.

**LE SALON DU LIVRE ET DU PAPIER ANCIEN** at the Porte de Champerret focuses on old books, posters, postcards, photos of all kinds, playing cards and letters, with more than 120 exhibitors. JOEL-GARCIA-ORGANISATION.FR

**LE SALON EMMAÜS** happens every year in June. This is the recycling and bargain-hunter trade show that encourages sustainable consumption. EMMAUS-FRANCE.ORG

For the fashionista, there's Paris **FASHION WEEK** of course. The *Mode à Paris* website gives schedules for the two haute couture and two ready-to-wear shows each year. To coincide with Fashion Week, four times a year **TRANOÏ** plays matchmaker to creativity and business. But it's more than just catwalks: there are installations, parties and fashion-related events around Paris. Twice a year, the high-visibility **WHO'S NEXT** show announces new trends in colours, materials and shapes, drawing on up-and-coming designers.
MODEAPARIS.COM / TRANOI.COM / WHOSNEXT.COM

During these intense periods of the trade shows, here are two places guaranteed to help you unwind and catch your breath: **ESPACE YON-KA** for a massage and the **HAMMAM PACHA** for a Turkish bath and a scrub.
ESPACE YON-KA: 39 RUE DE SÈVRES . 75006 . 01 45 44 39 79 . LESPACEYONKA.FR
HAMMAM PACHA: 17 RUE MAYET . 75006 . 01 43 06 55 55 . HAMMAMPACHA.COM

# *Festivals*

*Several festivals throughout the year showcase art and creativity and give you access to Parisian sites at quite surprising hours.*

Imagine wandering among paintings by Renoir and Monet after nightfall. **LA NUIT DES MUSÉES** is held every year in May. Most locations are open until midnight and offer concerts. NUITDESMUSEES.CULTURE.FR

During one **PARIS QUARTIER D'ÉTÉ** festival, I remember watching a dance concert at dawn in the middle of August in the Cour d'Honneur of Les Invalides. It was magical. For a month from mid-July to mid-August, the festival offers theatre in the gardens, live music and lots of concerts. It's a wonderful way to discover Paris.
QUARTIERDETE.COM

If you're in Paris on 5 and 6 October, make sure you follow the **LA NUIT BLANCHE** program. Throughout the night different artists take over iconic sites in Paris, making art accessible to all and making the most of urban spaces. Artist Sophie Calle took part in a memorable 2002 event, with visitors telling her stories while she lay in a bed on the top level of the Eiffel Tower.

And to help you keep up with all the cultural activities and special events, the city of Paris has launched a remarkably well-designed website, **QUE FAIRE À PARIS**.
QUEFAIRE.PARIS.FR

# Communicating

Paris is oddly under-equipped when it comes to wi-fi access, although the city has recently released a map showing 400 free wi-fi locations in parks, gardens, museums and metro stations: PARIS.FR/WIFI. The majority of new cafés also offer a free service. If you come to Paris and want to make a telephone call within France, certainly the most practical option is to buy a *bic® phone*, available for €29 from tobacconists, newsagents, supermarkets and hypermarkets. You have 30 minutes of calls valid for a month, 100 SMS messages and a charged battery. To call France from an international phone, don't forget to add the +33.

# Getting around

People walk and rush around a lot in Paris, the pace is fairly intense and Parisians are not always friendly, so it can feel quite hectic. I get around on foot, on the Métro or by bicycle, and sometimes by bus, which can be faster. The bus network is extensive.

Try cycling around Paris. The **VÉLIB'** hire stations are everywhere and operate 24/7. You can buy a day ticket for €1.70 or pay €8 for seven days. The first 30 minutes are free, then allow €1 for each additional half hour. If you're here for a longer period, become a member in advance on the Vélib' website. It's very practical and a great way to discover the city, especially in summer! Download the Vélib' phone app, which tells you where the nearest stations are to you and the availability of bikes.
EN.VELIB.PARIS.FR

**AUTO LIB'** has also been embraced by Parisians. The cars are available with or without a membership on presentation of a driving licence and you can book a vehicle up to 20 minutes in advance, and the same for a parking space. Without a membership, a day pass is free and you pay €9 per half hour of use. The weekly pass costs €10 and you pay €7 per half hour of use.
AUTOLIB.EU

There are remarkably few **TAXIS** in Paris; don't be surprised if occasionally you have to wait quite a while. If you need to order a taxi for the next morning between 7 and 9 am, make sure you do it well in advance the day before because they are often booked up. TAXISG7.FR or TAXIS-BLEUS.COM

There are some new taxi companies, including **LE CAB**, where you pay a fixed price based on the start and end point of your trip. You order the taxi using a phone app and the amount is debited directly from your account. It's best to book in advance.
LECAB.FR

Your **UBER** account also works in Paris!

If you plan to travel a lot by **BUS AND METRO**, zones 1 and 2 cover all of Paris. For a day out, buy a *Mobilis* ticket, which gives you unlimited bus and metro trips for €6.50. For a week, buy a *Navigo* pass, which gives you unlimited travel for €17.50. You'll find them in metro stations, along with a map of the different lines.
RATP.FR

# A weekend in Paris
## SEE AND DO A LOT IN A SHORT AMOUNT OF TIME

*FRIDAY EVENING.* Check into the hotel or apartment that you have carefully chosen in a centrally located arrondissement, say in the 10th. Head to **LE RICHER**— the restaurant doesn't take reservations, so wait at the bar with a glass of wine recommended by Charles. The elegant menu and ambience will be the perfect start to your weekend in Paris. It's a lively area and you can easily continue the evening by drifting over to **LE FANTÔME**, a bar a little further north in Rue de Paradis, where cocktails jostle with foosball.

*SATURDAY.* Depending on how you've fared from the night before, you'll ideally set out by 9 am to make the most of the day. Head on foot towards Rue du Nil to enjoy coffee and pancakes at **FRENCHIE TO GO** and check out the vegetables, cheeses and seafood at **TERROIRS D'AVENIR**.
Once you've had your fill, wander down the charming and lively Rue Montorgueil, turn left at Rue Étienne Marcel and find the metro station (Étienne Marcel). Take the train to the Saint-Ouen flea market at the end of line 4, Porte de Clignancourt. After you've made the rounds and your hunger has returned, you can have a bite on site at **MA COCOTTE** by the Marché Serpette or else head back towards the centre of Paris (allow 30 to 40 minutes). Take bus no. 85 by Rue Paul Bert. If the weather is fine, stay on the bus until it reaches its terminus (the Sorbonne) and enjoy a stroll in the **JARDIN DU LUXEMBOURG**, making your way to the Saint-Germain-des-Prés neighbourhood via the Rue de l'Odéon. If you haven't been lucky with the weather, get off at the Saint-Michel–Saint-Germain stop and head towards Rue des Quatre-Vents, where you can lunch at **LA CRÈMERIE** on burrata, smoked ham, terrine and a glass of red wine.

Take a stroll through the Saint-Germain neighbourhood, walk along the riverbanks, go via the Île de la Cité and don't miss **LA SAINTE-CHAPELLE**, a chapel hidden next to the Conciergerie. You can also make a reservation for a classical music concert held inside the chapel every Saturday (CLASSICTIC.COM). Make a quick trip back to the hotel to freshen up and put on your glad rags—you're in Paris, after all. For dinner, it's best to book in advance. Try **LA RÉGALADE SAINT-HONORÉ**, then take an evening promenade by the Louvre and see the Pyramide, avoiding the daytime crowds. **MON VIEIL AMI**, on Île Saint-Louis, is another restaurant in a dreamy setting. Parisians tend to go out more on Friday nights; Saturday nights are often reserved for dinners with friends at home.

*SUNDAY.* Take your time, get some croissants from the nearest bakery or go for a Vélib' ride if time permits. Head towards the area around Canal Saint-Martin, near the Jacques Bonsergent metro station. Rue Lucien Sampaix has three excellent options for brunch: **TUCK SHOP**, **BOB'S JUICE BAR** and **HOLYBELLY**. A little further north, in Rue de la Grange-aux-Belles, the **TEN BELLES** café makes excellent coffee and is in a perfect location. The shops around the canal open at about 2 pm: check out **ARTAZART**, at Quai de Valmy, and **LE CENTRE COMMERCIAL**, in Rue de Marseille. Another must is the Marais, at Saint Paul metro station. Most shops there open on Sundays. There'll be lots of people—it's a meeting place for fashionable Parisians. If it's raining, there's nothing better than seeing an old film in one of the many movie theatres in the 5th or 6th arrondissements. And of course there's always a must-see exhibition at **CENTQUATRE**, the **PALAIS DE TOKYO** or the **GRAND PALAIS**.

# A few hotels ...

For some time now, hotels have been popping up in Paris that display a passion for design and aesthetics. These new establishments often call on talented young interior designers who offer a more contemporary style, elegant yet accessible. Three of the following hotels are located in the 9th and 10th arrondissements, neighbourhoods that are undergoing a transformation and seeing the emergence of many promising new addresses.

## HÔTEL DU TEMPS

Revamped by Alix Thomsen from the *Thomsen Paris* clothing label, this hotel is a little jewel, fresh and bright, full of colour and patterns. Book a suite, if you can. Double rooms start at €160.

11 RUE DE MONTHOLON . 75009 . 01 47 70 37 16 . HOTEL-DU-TEMPS.FR . MÉTRO POISSONNIÈRE

## HÔTEL PARADIS

As the quote from Jules Renard in the window says, *'Add two letters to Paris, and you have Paradis'* (paradise). The hotel's interior designer was Dorothée Meilichzon, who also put her signature on *Café Pinson*, the *Compagnie des Vins Surnaturels* and *Beef Club*. About thirty different types of wallpaper were used to decorate the rooms. Double rooms start at €90.

41 RUE DES PETITES ÉCURIES . 75010 . 01 45 23 08 22 . HOTELPARADISPARIS.COM . MÉTRO BONNE NOUVELLE

## HÔTEL DE NELL

Located in the 9th arrondissement, this highly regarded five-star establishment owes much to the expertise of designer Jean-Michel Willmote and restaurateur Bruno Doucet, the chef at *La Régalade*. The restaurant *La Régalade Conservatoire* is attached to the hotel.

7–9 RUE DU CONSERVATOIRE . 75009 . 01 44 83 83 60 . HOTELDENELL.COM . MÉTRO BONNE NOUVELLE

## HÔTEL JULES ET JIM

This is a beautiful modern hotel in Rue des Gravilliers in the 3rd arrondissement. Rooms start at €200. The hotel features an outdoor fireplace.

11 RUE DES GRAVILLIERS . 75003 . 01 44 54 13 13 . HOTELJULESETJIM.COM . MÉTRO ARTS ET MÉTIERS

# LE SERGENT RECRUTEUR

# A few restaurants ...

*There are so many it's impossible to fit them onto one page. Here is a small selection of the ones I have a particular soft spot for.*

**LE RICHER**, for the elegance of its dishes and its pricing. There are no reservations, but the wait is not too long and it's open every day. Entrée–main or main–dessert from €30, without drinks.
2 RUE RICHER . 75009 . MÉTRO CADET

**COINSTOT VINO**, for its fine ingredients and warm hospitality. It offers natural wines, boards of charcuterie or smoked fish and hot dishes. Less than €45 a head.
26 BIS PASSAGE DES PANORAMAS . 75002 . 01 44 82 08 54 . COINSTOT-VINO.COM . MÉTRO BOURSE

**LE SERGENT RECRUTEUR**, for its incredible location, sumptuous décor and the superb cuisine of Antonin Bonnet, who trained under Michel Bras. More than €50 per head.
41 RUE SAINT-LOUIS-EN-L'ILE . 75004 . 01 43 54 75 42 . LESERGENTRECRUTEUR.FR . MÉTRO PONT MARIE

**CAFFÈ DEI CIOPPI**, for delicious Italian food. This restaurant has a very small dining room, so it's best to book. In summer, ask for a table on the terrace. €40 for a meal.
159 RUE DU FAUBOURG-SAINT-ANTOINE . 75011 . 01 43 46 10 14 . MÉTRO LEDRU ROLLIN

**L'ÉBAUCHOIR**, for its produce-driven cuisine, a few steps from the *Marché d'Aligre*. Less than €40.
43 RUE DE CITEAUX . 75012 . 01 43 42 49 31 . LEBAUCHOIR.COM . MÉTRO FAIDHERBE-CHALIGNY

**KUNITORAYA**, for its udon noodles made in-house. A real treat.
1 RUE VILLEDO . 75001 . 01 47 03 33 65 . KUNITORAYA.COM . MÉTRO PALAIS ROYAL–MUSÉE DU LOUVRE

**LA CRÈMERIE**, for its burrata and wine cellar.
9 RUE DES QUATRE-VENTS . 75006 . 01 43 54 99 30 . LACREMERIE.FR . MÉTRO ODÉON

**CHEZ NENESSE**, for good traditional French cuisine. From €25.
17 RUE DE SAINTONGE . 75003 . 01 42 78 46 49 . MÉTRO RÉPUBLIQUE

**CAILLEBOTTE**, for its bistro spirit with a modern flavour.
8 RUE HIPPOLYTE LEBAS . 75009 . 01 53 20 88 70 . MÉTRO NOTRE-DAME-DE-LORETTE

**SEPTIME**, for its setting and the wonderful cuisine of Bertrand Grébaut. Set menu for €55.
80 RUE DE CHARONNE . 75011 . 01 43 67 38 29 . SEPTIME-CHARONNE.FR . MÉTRO CHARONNE

*For more ideas the* Fooding *website is a good starting point.* LEFOODING.COM

# A few indulgences ...

*One of Paris' highlights is its pastries and other sweet treats. This is another long list.*

*A GOOD CROISSANT?* Can be found in many Parisian bakeries, but especially **SÉBASTIEN GAUDARD**. The store is superb, as are its pastries and croissants.
22 RUE DES MARTYRS . 75009 . 01 71 18 24 70 . SEBASTIENGAUDARD.FR . MÉTRO NOTRE-DAME-DE-LORETTE

*TEA AND CAKE?* The **LOIR DANS LA THÉIÈRE**.
3 RUE DES ROSIERS . 75004 . 01 42 72 90 61 . MÉTRO SAINT-PAUL

*A HOT CHOCOLATE?* **JEAN-PAUL HÉVIN'S CHOCOLATE BAR**.
231 RUE SAINT-HONORÉ . 75001 . 01 55 35 35 96 . JEANPAULHEVIN.COM. MÉTRO TUILERIES

*GLUTEN-FREE?* **HELMUT NEWCAKE**.
36 RUE BICHAT . 75010 . 09 82 59 00 39 . HELMUTNEWCAKE.COM . MÉTRO GONCOURT

*ICE CREAM?* There is, of course, **BERTHILLON**, on the lovely Île Saint-Louis.
BERTHILLON: 29–31 RUE SAINT-LOUIS EN L'ÎLE . 75004 . 01 43 54 31 61 . BERTHILLON.FR . MÉTRO CITÉ

*A MILLE-FEUILLE?* **ANGELINA** makes one to die for, just like their Mont Blanc.
226 RUE DE RIVOLI . 75001 . 01 42 60 82 00 . ANGELINA-PARIS.FR . MÉTRO TUILERIES

*CHOUX PUFFS?* At **POPELINI**, the ones with salted butter caramel are delicious.
29 RUE DEBELLEYME . 75003 . 01 44 61 31 44 . MÉTRO SAINT-SÉBASTIEN-FROISSARD
44 RUE DES MARTYRS . 75009 . 01 42 81 35 79 . MÉTRO NOTRE-DAME-DE-LORETTE . POPELINI.COM

*CHIFFON CAKE?* **PÂTISSERIE CIEL**, for the lightest of cakes.
3 RUE MONGE . 75005 . 01 43 29 40 78 . PATISSERIE-CIEL.COM . MÉTRO MAUBERT MUTUALITÉ

*MACARONS?* **LADURÉE** or **PIERRE HERMÉ**.
LADURÉE: 16–18 RUE ROYALE . 75008 . 01 42 60 21 79 . MÉTRO CONCORDE
21 RUE BONAPARTE 75006 . 01 44 07 64 87 . MÉTRO SAINT-GERMAIN-DES-PRÉS . LADUREE.COM
PIERRE HERMÉ: 72 RUE BONAPARTE . 75006 . 01 43 54 47 77
185 RUE DE VAUGIRARD . 75015 . 01 47 83 89 97 . MÉTRO PASTEUR
39 AVENUE DE L'OPÉRA . 75002 . 01 43 54 47 77 . MÉTRO OPÉRA . PIERREHERME.COM

*MERINGUES?* From **MERVEILLEUX**, which has five Paris stores.
94 RUE SAINT-DOMINIQUE . 75007 . 01 47 53 91 34 . AUXMERVEILLEUX.COM
MÉTRO LA TOUR-MAUBOURG

*CHOCOLATE TRUFFLES?* **LA MAISON DU CHOCOLAT** has the best. There are several stores in Paris.
8 BOULEVARD DE LA MADELEINE . 75009 . 01 47 42 86 52 . LAMAISONDUCHOCOLAT.COM
MÉTRO MADELEINE

*CHOCOLATE BARS?* **LA MANUFACTURE ALAIN DUCASSE** is a magnificent place and the chocolate is made on site, from scratch, right from the bean.
40 RUE DE LA ROQUETTE . 75011 . 01 48 05 82 86 . LECHOCOLAT-ALAINDUCASSE.COM . MÉTRO BASTILLE

*JAMS?* **LA CHAMBRE AUX CONFITURES** has a fabulous selection of original flavours.
9 RUE DES MARTYRS . 75009 . 01 71 73 43 77 . MÉTRO NOTRE-DAME-DE-LORETTE
60 RUE VIEILLE-DU-TEMPLE . 75003 . 01 79 25 53 58 . MÉTRO SAINT-PAUL
LACHAMBREAUXCONFITURES.COM

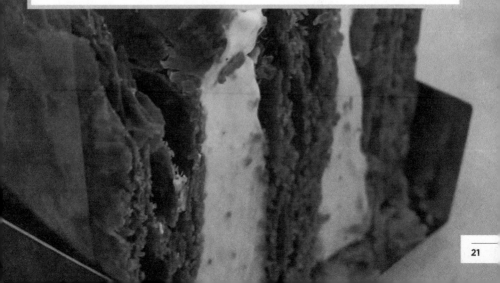

# A few bars ...

*In Paris, the ritual of the aperitif is widely observed. People often meet after work in bars or wine cellars that offer charcuterie boards and little morsels to nibble on.*

**LE GARDE ROBE**, for its authenticity. Dishes from €12 to €15.
41 RUE DE L'ARBRE SEC . 75001 . 01 49 26 90 60 . MÉTRO CHATELET

**L'ENTRÉE DES ARTISTES**, for its cocktails and small plates.
8 RUE DE CRUSSOL . 75011 . 09 50 99 67 11 . MÉTRO FILLES DU CALVAIRE

**VERJUS**, for the intimate feel of its vaulted cellar. Tapas from €7, drinks €6 to €12.
52 RUE DE RICHELIEU . 75001 . 01 42 97 54 40 . VERJUSPARIS.COM . MÉTRO PYRAMIDES

**AUX DEUX AMIS**, for its friendly atmosphere. From €16 to €35.
45 RUE OBERKAMPF . 75011 . 01 58 30 38 13 . MÉTRO PARMENTIER

**BONES,** for its bar menu, its house-made products, such as the bread and butter, and the wine selection. Plates at the bar from €4 to €30.
43 RUE GODEFROY CAVAIGNAC . 75011 . 09 80 75 32 08 . BONESPARIS.COM . MÉTRO VOLTAIRE

**L'AVANT COMPTOIR**, for Yves Camdeborde's *pintxos*—a type of tapas from northern Spain—and the steady throng of people. Plates from €3 to €10.
3 CARREFOUR DE L'ODÉON . 75006 . 01 44 27 07 97 . HOTEL-PARIS-RELAIS-SAINT-GERMAIN.COM
MÉTRO ODÉON

**LE ROSA BONHEUR**, set in the Parc des Buttes Chaumont, for the perfect place to go in summer. Little baskets of charcuterie and cheeses for less than €15.
2 AVENUE DES CASCADES . 75019 . 01 42 00 00 45 . ROSABONHEUR.FR . MÉTRO BOTZARIS

*And later, for a cocktail:*

**EXPERIMENTAL COCKTAIL CLUB**, inspired by New York and just perfect.
37 RUE SAINT-SAUVEUR . 75002 . 01 45 08 88 09 . EXPERIMENTALCOCKTAILCLUB.FR . MÉTRO SENTIER

**ARTISAN** offers cocktails and tapas.
14 RUE BOCHART DE SARON . 75009 . 01 48 74 65 38 . ARTISAN-BAR.FR . MÉTRO ANVERS

**GLASS,** for beer and hot dogs.
7 RUE FROCHOT . 75009 . 09 80 72 98 83 . GLASSPARIS.COM . MÉTRO PIGALLE

**SHANGRI-LA HOTEL BAR**, for its elegance and exotic cocktails.
10 AVENUE D'IÉNA . 75016 . 01 53 67 19 98 . SHANGRI-LA.COM/PARIS . MÉTRO IÉNA

**THE LITTLE RED DOOR**, a little hidden-away gem.
60 RUE CHARLOT . 75003 . 01 42 71 19 32 . LRDPARIS.COM . MÉTRO OBERKAMPF

**BAR LE COQ**, for its British-inspired cocktails.
12 RUE DU CHÂTEAU D'EAU . 75010 . 01 42 40 85 68 . MÉTRO JACQUES BONSERGENT

# A few (good) cafés ...

*The popularity of a Parisian café terrace is usually a measure of its location, like the terraces of Café Le Nemours by the Palais-Royal or Bar du Marché on Rue de Seine. But a café's popularity is not always a reflection of the quality of its espresso.*

*The trend of the 'flat white' has finally reached Paris and the French ones now rival those produced by their English-speaking counterparts. Coffee has been roasted in Paris for a long time by the Verlet cafés, especially at Coffelia in Rue Condorcet and more recently at Café Lomi, Café Coutume and the Brûlerie de Belleville. New places are opening at a rapid pace. Here are some where the coffee is excellent.*

**KB** 62 RUE DES MARTYRS . 75009 . 01 56 92 12 41 . MÉTRO PIGALLE

**BOOT CAFÉ** 19 RUE DU PONT-AUX-CHOUX . 75003 . 01 73 70 14 57 . LEBOOTCAFE.FR
MÉTRO SAINT-SEBASTIEN–FROISSART

**TEN BELLES** 10 RUE DE LA GRANGE-AUX-BELLES . 75010 . 01 42 40 90 78 . TENBELLES.COM
MÉTRO COLONEL FABIEN

**LA CAFÉOTHÈQUE** 52 RUE DE L'HÔTEL DE VILLE . 75004 . 01 53 01 83 84
LACAFEOTHEQUE.COM . MÉTRO PONT MARIE

**HOLYBELLY** 19 RUE LUCIEN SAMPAIX . 75010 . 09 73 60 13 64 . MÉTRO JACQUES BONSERGENT

**TUCK SHOP** 13 RUE LUCIEN SAMPAIX . 75010 . 09 80 72 95 40 . MÉTRO JACQUES BONSERGENT

**COUTUME CAFÉ** 47 RUE DE BABYLONE . 75007 . 01 45 51 50 47 . MÉTRO SAINT-FRANCOIS-XAVIER

**COUTUME LAB** 4 RUE DU BOULOI . 75001 . 01 45 51 50 47 . MÉTRO LOUVRE-RIVOLI

**FRAGMENTS** 76 RUE DES TOURNELLES . 75003 . MÉTRO CHEMIN VERT

**CAFÉ LOMI** 3 TER RUE MARCADET . 75018 . 09 80 39 56 24 . CAFELOMI.COM . MÉTRO MARX DORMOY

**TÉLESCOPE** 5 RUE VILLEDO . 75001 . 01 42 61 33 14 . TELESCOPECAFE.COM . MÉTRO PYRAMIDES

**LE LOUSTIC** 40 RUE CHAPON . 75003 . 09 80 31 07 06 . MÉTRO ARTS ET MÉTIERS

**LE BAL CAFÉ** 6 IMPASSE DE LA DÉFENSE . 75018 . 01 44 70 75 51 . MÉTRO PLACE DE CLICHY

**THE BROKEN ARM** 12 RUE PERRÉE . 75003 . 01 44 61 53 60 . THE-BROKEN-ARM.COM . MÉTRO TEMPLE

**BRÛLERIE DE BELLEVILLE** 10 RUE PRADIER . 75019 . 09 83 75 60 80 . MÉTRO PYRÉNÉES

**COFFÉLIA** 45 RUE CONDORCET . 75009 . 01 40 16 04 68 . COFFELIA.FR . MÉTRO ANVERS

**CAFÉ VERLET** 256 RUE SAINT-HONORÉ . 75001 . 01 42 60 67 39 . VERLET.FR
MÉTRO PALAIS ROYAL–MUSÉE DU LOUVRE

**FONDATION CAFÉ** 16 RUE DUPETIT-THOUARS . 75003 . MÉTRO TEMPLE

**CAFÉ CRAFT** 24 RUE DES VINAIGRIERS . 75010 . 01 40 35 90 77 . CAFE-CRAFT.COM
MÉTRO JACQUES BONSERGENT

# To market, to market ...

*Every neighbourhood in Paris has its own market, where you'll find fresh produce, fruit and vegetables, cheese, meat, fish, flowers ... These are my favourites.*

**MARCHÉ D'ALIGRE** Part of the market is covered, the square is surrounded by cafés and you'll find the wonderful *Graineterie du Marché* at number 8.
PLACE D'ALIGRE . 75012 . MÉTRO LEDRU-ROLLIN . OPEN EVERY DAY FROM 9 AM TO 1 PM THEN FROM 4 PM TO 7.30 PM

**MARCHÉ D'ANVERS** A small market but with quality products including Provibio, an organic greengrocer and very good goat cheeses from M. Gaillardin.
PLACE D'ANVERS . 75009 . MÉTRO ANVERS . FRIDAY FROM 3 PM TO 8 PM

**MARCHÉ COUVERT DES ENFANTS ROUGES** This is a good place for lunch in the Marais; the Moroccan food is particularly delicious.
39 RUE DE BRETAGNE . 75003 . MÉTRO TEMPLE . OPEN TUESDAY TO SUNDAY FROM 8.30 AM TO 7.30 PM

**MARCHÉ DE LA PLACE DES FÊTES** A huge variety of beautiful, exotic products.
PLACE DES FÊTES . 75019 . MÉTRO PLACE DES FÊTES . TUESDAY AND FRIDAY FROM 7 AM TO 2.30 PM SUNDAY FROM 7 AM TO 3 PM

**MARCHÉ DU PRÉSIDENT WILSON** A magnificent market, though quite expensive. Includes the superb fresh produce of market gardener Joël Thiebault.
AVENUE DU PRÉSIDENT WILSON . 75016 . BETWEEN RUE DEBROUSSE AND PLACE D'IÉNA . MÉTRO ALMA MARCEAU . OPEN WEDNESDAY AND SATURDAY FROM 7 AM TO 2.30 PM

**MARCHÉ BIOLOGIQUE DES BATIGNOLLES** All organic, all fantastic!
34 BOULEVARD DES BATIGNOLLES . 75017 . MÉTRO ROME . EVERY SATURDAY FROM 9 AM TO 3 PM

**MARCHÉ RASPAIL** A very large market during the week that transforms into an organic market on Sundays.

BOULEVARD RASPAIL, BETWEEN RUE DU CHERCHE-MIDI AND RUE DE RENNES . 75006 . MÉTRO RASPAIL
TUESDAY AND FRIDAY FROM 7 AM TO 2 PM, SUNDAY FROM 9 AM TO 3 PM

**TERROIRS D'AVENIR** The people behind this company were inspired by the Slow Food movement. They source high-quality produce from small French, and some foreign, producers. Since 2008 they have been supplying a selection of fine Parisian restaurants, such as *Frenchie* and *Le Galopin*. Then they had the brilliant idea of opening three shops on Rue du Nil: a butcher, a greengrocer and a fishmonger. It's a street that no foodie should miss. While you're there, try the delicious pancakes at *Frenchie To Go*—without a doubt, the best in Paris.

TERROIRS D'AVENIR: 6, 7, 8 RUE DU NIL . 75002 . 01 45 08 48 80 . MÉTRO SENTIER . TUESDAY TO
FRIDAY 10 AM TO 2.30 PM AND 4.30 PM TO 9 PM, SATURDAY 9 AM TO 9 PM, SUNDAY 9 AM TO 2 PM
FRENCHIE TO GO: 9 RUE DU NIL . 75002 . 01 40 39 96 19 . FRENCHIETOGO.COM . MÉTRO SENTIER

# 01

## CONTEMPORARY INSPIRATION

Be inspired by this selection of the city's concept stores, trendsetters and newsmakers, creative designers, style alchemists and image-makers. You won't find any shrinking violets here!

*Natural cork* stools ●

pattern and *more pattern*

● a *transparent* acrylic

coffee table ● *copper*

● a *wall dresser* in a

gradation of colours ●

*sycamore* lampshades ●

textured *marble platters*

● an *illuminated mirror*

creating another dimension

● *glass coat-pegs* like

*bubbles* about

to *float* away ● *inspiration*

and *colour*

# Sarah Lavoine

Architect and interior designer Sarah Lavoine sets a high benchmark in the field of decoration. At the helm of two stores, she adapts her modern, clean and simple style to various high-end projects across Paris and is creative director of the new **CFOC** concept store. The *Sarah Lavoine* style is grounded in an intelligent mastery of colour and a taste for simple, warm and contemporary shapes.

9 RUE SAINT-ROCH . 75001 . 01 42 96 34 35 . MÉTRO TUILERIES

28 RUE DU BAC . 75007 . 01 42 86 00 35 . MÉTRO RUE DU BAC

SARAHLAVOINE.COM

1*st* . 7*th*
. Map p. 260
~ p. 270

*If you find yourself on Rue Saint-Roch, then you're just a few steps from the famous Paris department store* **Colette**. *Continuing along towards the Jardin des Tuileries, make sure you visit* **107RIVOLI**, *the boutique of the Musée des Arts Décoratifs. Hidden inside is a superb bookshop devoted to decorative arts, photography, graphics and textile design. You will also find many contemporary objects and jewellery.*

# Kann Design

Located in the vibrant Rue des Vinaigriers near the Canal Saint-Martin, the designers at *Kann Design* specialise in furniture inspired by the 1950s. Armchairs, sofas, coffee tables and shelves are made by artisans in Lebanon. The direct relationship between designer and producer allows them to set more affordable prices. Check out the *Kora* range of fifties' chairs and sofas.

28 RUE DES VINAIGRIERS . 75010 . 09 53 40 86 98

KANNDESIGN.COM . MÉTRO JACQUES BONSERGENT

$10^{th}$
*Map p. 274*

*Rue des Vinaigriers is chock-full of interesting shops that shouldn't be missed. **Café Craft**, designed by the Pool studio, is at number 24. It has great coffee and a workspace. Don't miss the **Loft design by** store at number 29—it's a beautiful space that was previously home to the lovely **Galerie Végétale**. The **Loft** brand has developed its first fine food store there. The **Sol Semilla** 'superfoods' store (berries, seeds and food powders) is at number 23. **La Piñata** makes fabulous piñatas and sells games for children. For lovers of old shops, **Jean-Marc Poursin**'s store at number 35 is a must-see. This beautiful shop, dating back to 1891, specialises in buckles and straps for saddlery and leather goods.*

# Portobello

In Rue du Roi de Sicile, a few steps from Rue des Rosiers, *Portobello* offers a wide range of fabrics, including beautiful washed linens in rich shades, suitable for the bedroom as well as the living room. *Portobello* produces and distributes sofas and shelving by designer *Rébecca Felcey*. You'll also find the innovative creations of the *Petite Friture* designers there.

32 RUE DU ROI DE SICILE . 75004 . 01 42 72 27 74
PORTOBELLO-DECORATION.FR . MÉTRO SAINT-PAUL

*4*th
Map p. 266

# Colonel

Created in 2010 by Isabelle Gilles and Yann Poncelet, the *Colonel* label and shop offers limited series of objects and furniture designed by the duo and produced by French artisans. Beechwood tables with simple lines, lampshades made from colourful fabrics or sycamore ply and armchairs inspired by the camping chairs of the 1960s create a universe that's fresh and contemporary. Alongside these colourful designs are fine names, such as Denmark's *HAY* and Belgium's *Nuée*.

14 AVENUE RICHERAND . 75010 . 01 83 89 69 22 . MONCOLONEL.FR
MÉTRO JACQUES BONSERGENT

*10$^{th}$*
*Map p.274*

*This shop is close to the Canal Saint-Martin. You're next door to* **Le Comptoir Général** *and the* **Ten Belles** *café. Check the map on page 274 so you don't miss anything.*

# Galeries Sentou

The *Sentou* name now extends to three superb Paris stores and a showroom reserved for professionals. The brand is run by Pierre Romanet and it has become a benchmark for colour and style both in Paris and abroad. *Sentou* is above all a producer and distributor of furniture and objects, favouring block colours and simple shapes. Go to *Sentou* for their *Coogee* sofa, the *Mud Australia* tableware, the *Isabelle* chairs and the *Le Deun* lamps.

29 RUE FRANÇOIS MIRON . 75004 . 01 42 78 50 60 . MÉTRO SAINT-PAUL

26 BOULEVARD RASPAIL . 75007 . 01 45 49 00 05 . MÉTRO SÈVRES-BABYLONE

112 BOULEVARD DE COURCELLES . 75017 . 01 82 83 52 90

MÉTRO COURCELLES . SENTOU.FR

4th . 7th
Map p. 266
– p. 270

*The store on Rue François Miron is opposite **Izraël**, an Aladdin's cave of a grocery store that has spices and more from around the globe. 30 Rue François Miron . 75004*

# Marcel By

A new design house that has met with great success, *Marcel By* manufactures and sells furniture, represents young designers and highlights the artisans they work with. At *Marcel By* you can spot *Stephan Lanez's* Russian candle jars, the Bambi chair of *Noé Duchaufour-Lawrance* or *Samuel Accoceberry's* mirrors.

28 RUE SAINT-CLAUDE . 75003 . 01 57 40 80 77 . MARCELBY.FR

MÉTRO SAINT-SÉBASTIEN–FROISSART

3rd
*Map p.264*

FR 66, *another excellent French furniture maker and distributor riding a wave, is 15 minutes away via Rue Vieille-du-Temple and Rue Sainte-Croix-de-la-Bretonnerie. 25 Rue du Renard . 75004*

# Maison M

Created by lifestyle journalist Carolina Tossan-Covillard in autumn 2013, *Maison M* is organised like a magazine. The display window, much like a cover photo, showcases the trends and inside the themes change every month. From the lovely *Papier Tigre* stationery, a collaboration with the *Minakani Lab* wallpaper designers, to various Danish and French brands—some previously unseen in France—it's a discerning selection that is regularly updated.

25 RUE DE BOURGOGNE . 75007 . 01 47 53 07 74 . MAISONMPARIS.COM
MÉTRO SOLFÉRINO

*7ᵗʰ*
*Map p.270*

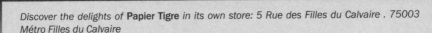

*Discover the delights of* **Papier Tigre** *in its own store: 5 Rue des Filles du Calvaire . 75003 Métro Filles du Calvaire*

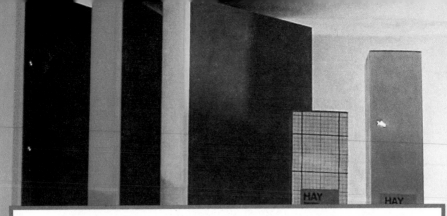

# Home Autour du Monde

Set up in the early 1980s by Serge Bensimon—a keen traveller and a key figure in the Paris decorating and lifestyle scene—the *Home Autour du Monde* store sells the now-famous *Bensimon* tennis shoes alongside furniture and design objects over two floors. There's lots of colour and a well-judged contemporary selection, including *Lampe Gras* lamps, decorative objects, textiles and home fragrances, which all form part of the identity of the brand. After more than thirty years, *Bensimon* is more than a fashion brand, it's a lifestyle, with stores in many locations.

Serge Bensimon was also the man behind **ARTAZART**, the unmissable Parisian bookstore specialising in graphic design and photography, and promoting young talent. In 2009, **GALLERY S. BENSIMON** in Rue de Turenne was born, showcasing designers, artists and artisans who in turn present their vision of the world through objects and furniture.

12 RUE DES FRANCS BOURGEOIS . 75003 . 01 42 77 16 18 . BENSIMON.COM

MÉTRO SAINT-PAUL

ARTAZART: 83 QUAI DE VALMY . 75010 . 01 40 40 24 00 . ARTAZART.COM

MÉTRO JACQUES BONSERGENT

*3rd*
*Map p. 264*

# Persona Grata

This is the store to come to for a large selection of *Tolix* furniture. Famous since 1934 thanks to its iconic Model A metal chair, *Tolix* has since expanded its range of French-made industrial-style furniture. It now offers benches, stools, one-door cabinets, three-door cabinets, shelves, desks for children and more in a range of fun, bright colours.

71 BD DE SÉBASTOPOL . 75002 . 01 42 33 15 15 . PERSONA-GRATA.COM

MÉTRO ÉTIENNE MARCEL

2nd
Map p.262

# Mona Market

Mona Market is a whole universe of homewares showcased over two levels. Step into a complete kitchen, bedroom or bathroom, presented as if ready to be used. It offers a wide range of interesting brands. I go there for the *Chez Honoré* tableware collections and pretty hanging and standing lamps from *Paris au Mois d'Août*, entirely handmade in coloured fabrics.

4 RUE COMMINES . 75003 . 01 42 78 80 04 . MONAMARKET.COM

MÉTRO SAINT-SÉBASTIEN–FROISSART

3rd
Map p. 264

At number 1 Rue Commines is **Le Mary Céleste**, *a cocktail bar. Sticking with the maritime theme, try their fish and seafood plates.* LEMARYCELESTE.COM

# India Mahdavi

The list of India Mahdavi's projects, both in Paris and abroad, is a long one: *Café Français* in Place de la Bastille, chef Jean-François Piège's *Thoumieux* restaurant and *Hélène Darroze* restaurant in London to name a few.

India Mahdavi set up her creative headquarters in Rue Las Cases, as well as two sales outlets: the showroom at number 3 for furniture and the *petits objets* boutique at number 19 offering a selection of home accessories—cushions, vases, trays, ceramics—that represent the exotic, colourful and geometric universe of this architect and designer.

PETITS OBJETS: 19 RUE LAS CASES . 75007 . 01 45 55 88 88
SHOWROOM #3: 3 RUE LAS CASES . 75007 . 01 45 55 67 67
INDIA-MAHDAVI.COM . MÉTRO SOLFÉRINO

$7^{th}$
Map p. 270

50

# The Collection

*The Collection* is the exclusive Paris distributor for a range of objects, wallpapers and furniture by French and foreign designers. The small team is passionate about the artists it represents. Find embroidered wallpaper by *Tracy Kendall*, *3D* decorative wall pieces, *MINT Light Living* furniture made in Latvia and incredible creations from *Little Owl Design*.

33 RUE DE POITOU . 75003 . 01 42 77 04 20 . THECOLLECTION.FR

MÉTRO SAINT-SÉBASTIEN – FROISSART

3rd
Map p.264

# 02

## TEXTILES

Paris' furnishing fabric designers are highly regarded. Smaller independent stores can offer more personalised ranges, in natural fibres, often crafted by hand using traditional weaving techniques. This means you're likely to find a more individual and precious product. Textiles, Paris style.

Linen jacquard
contemporary cotton
canvas silk, wool
and cashmere exotic
plant fibres ecru
bold hues stripes
one-off fabrics
handmade, pastel shades
tweed water hyacinth
embroidery deep indigos
home furnishings
comfort

# Caravane Chambre 19

Two *Caravane* stores face each other on Rue Saint-Nicolas. *Chambre 19* is quite spectacular, firstly because of its interior setting—a gigantic palm casts shadows on the sofas beneath the glass ceiling—then because of its regularly changing displays and finally, because of the objects it sells. The colours and materials are always perfectly brought together in a warm and contemporary style. *Caravane* takes chances with luminous block yellows and fresh sea greens and offers quality products inspired by other places and mostly made in France. The fabrics themselves come from India, where traditional techniques are preserved and applied to more contemporary designs. Apart from the *Caravane* range, you'll find many products in the stores purchased on various trips abroad, such as the beaten metal basins with leather handles from Egypt, ancient coloured paddles from the Philippines and metal light bulbs. A third store, **CARAVANE LA MAISON**, is in the 6th arrondissemont.

19 RUE SAINT-NICOLAS . 75012 . 01 53 02 96 96 . CARAVANE.FR
MÉTRO LEDRU-ROLLIN

*12th*

# C M O

Marianne Oudin, who gave *C M O* its name, specialises in fabrics made from plant fibres—abacá, hemp, ramie, vetiver and pineapple fibres. In her shop in the centre of the 'Japanese quarter' you'll also find different woven materials—paper, water hyacinth and rattan. From cushions to curtains, Marianne Oudin also creates custom-made pieces to suit your own preferences.

5 RUE CHABANAIS . 75002 . 01 40 20 45 98 . CMOPARIS.COM
MÉTRO PYRAMIDES

*2nd*
Map p.262

housses, canapé, tenture murale...) jusqu'à la pose.
– Une collection de tringles réalisée selon vos dimensions et disponible en plusieurs finitions.
– Un site internet de vente en ligne proposant une grande partie des tissus proposés à la boutique ainsi que les produits finis et accessoires.
– Un service de « recherche textile » pour répondre à des demandes particulières (hôtellerie, tissus techniques...)

## QUI ?

Charlotte de La Grandière, styliste pour la presse déco, scénographe de vitrines et directrice artistique pour divers catalogue, a souhaité, en créant Rue Hérold, décomplexer l'approche du tissu haut de gamme et faire découvrir ou redécouvrir les belles matières.

## COMMENT ?

– En le rendant accessible et disponible à tous.
– En cherchant le meilleur rapport qualité-prix.
– Par un lieu épuré et fonctionnel, sans accroche « déco », où l'offre est clairement visible et dont le propos essentiel reste le tissu, les matières et les couleurs.
– Par une approche humoristique, fraîche et légère (Antinde, Abdo, Charivari, Dilirambique... pour le nom des tissus).
– Par une image et un graphisme simples et réfléchis.

– A curtain rod collection custom made to specific measures, available in different finishes.
– A web store proposing most of the fabrics available in store, as well as the 'take-away' goods and accessories.
– A 'fabric search' service to answer specific demands (hotels, technical textiles...)

## WHO?

Charlotte de La Grandière, stylist for decoration magazines, window display scenographer and art director for diverse catalogues, wished to deconsecrate the high quality fabric's approach and help to discover or re-discover beautiful materials.

## THE MEANS?

– By making it more accessible and available to everyone.
– By offering the best price/quality ratio.
– By presenting in a refined and functional space, with no eye-catching decorations, where products are easily identifiable in an offer centred on fabrics, materials and colours.
– With an humoristic fresh and light approach (Airbag, Abdo, Extra, Drink... as fabric's name).
– Through an image and graphics both simple and well-thought.

# Rue Herold

The space is beautiful, white, simple and graphic and seems to get straight to the point: selling beautiful fabrics at affordable prices. Charlotte de la Grandière, an enthusiastic and creative prop stylist, is behind this project. She selects the different fabrics: striped, plain, indigo, white and ecru linens, dusty pink linen-wool blends, beautiful cottons—natural materials for the most part. Fabric is sold by the metre and cut before your eyes—heavy bolts of fabric tumble down, material flies across a big table and scissors crisply get to work.

8 RUE HÉROLD . 75001 . 01 42 33 66 56 . RUEHEROLD.FR

MÉTRO PALAIS-ROYAL

1$^{st}$

Map p. 260

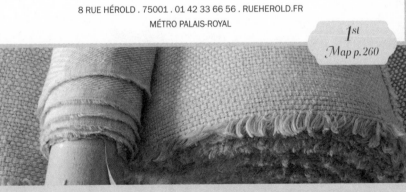

*You are two doors from the superb store* **L'Éclaireur.** *Press the intercom button and prepare to be surprised. (Hint: fashion heaven!) 10 Rue Hérold . 75001 . 01 40 41 09 89 . LECLAIREUR.COM*

# Kilim Ada

A kilim is a woven wool carpet from the Middle East, the Caucasus and Central Asia. Made in keeping with nomadic traditions, each kilim is a one-off inspiration with its own style, the patterns representing a kind of writing. *Kilim Ada* is one of the carpet pioneers in France and has been collecting traditional carpets from the most remote corners of the Middle East and Central Asia since 1985. For some time it's also been designing more contemporary-style carpets using the same traditional weaving techniques.

52 RUE DES ARCHIVES . 75004 . 01 42 78 03 02 . MÉTRO HÔTEL DE VILLE
34 RUE DES ÉCOLES . 75005 . 01 43 29 54 77 . MÉTRO MAUBERT-MUTUALITÉ
KILIMS.FR

4th . 5th
*Map p. 266*

# Lindell and Co

Gabrielle is Swedish and has lived in India. The cushions and carpets she sells in her little store are all meticulously hand-embroidered in Kashmir and are her own designs and collections. The colours she uses are bold and modern—greens, straw yellows, turquoises and reds.

14 RUE DU GRAND PRIEURÉ . 75011 . 01 43 57 43 42
LINDELLANDCO.COM . MÉTRO OBERKAMPF

11<sup>th</sup>
Map p.276

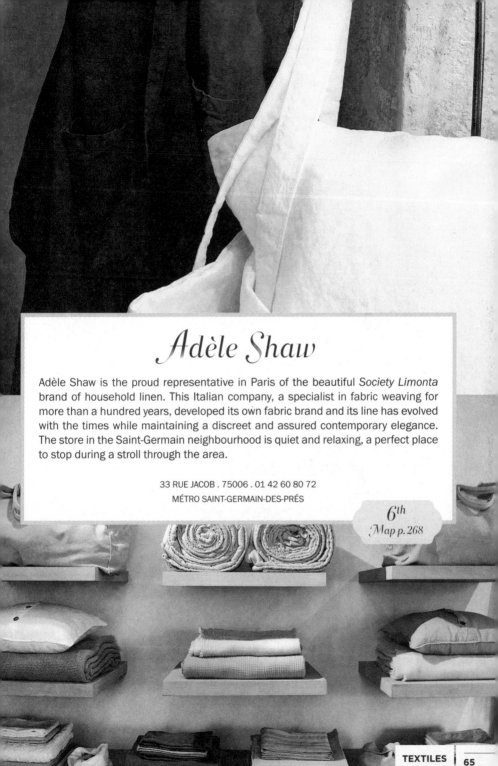

# Adèle Shaw

Adèle Shaw is the proud representative in Paris of the beautiful *Society Limonta* brand of household linen. This Italian company, a specialist in fabric weaving for more than a hundred years, developed its own fabric brand and its line has evolved with the times while maintaining a discreet and assured contemporary elegance. The store in the Saint-Germain neighbourhood is quiet and relaxing, a perfect place to stop during a stroll through the area.

33 RUE JACOB . 75006 . 01 42 60 80 72
MÉTRO SAINT-GERMAIN-DES-PRÉS

$6^{th}$
Map p. 268

# La Soie Disante

I discovered *La Soie Disante* when I was looking for the superb indigo-dyed fabrics of Aboubakar Fofana in Paris. The store, which carries many textile designers, sometimes offers creations from this Malian textile artist. The fabrics at *La Soie Disante* are sourced from Africa, Anatolia, Turkey ... It attracts numerous collectors looking for exclusive and original pieces.

36 RUE DE VERNEUIL . 75007 . 01 42 61 23 44
MÉTRO RUE DU BAC

7th
Map p. 270

*Continue along Rue de Verneuil towards Rue du Bac. Singer Serge Gainsbourg's home is a little further along. The graffiti-covered house is hard to miss.*

DREYFUS
DÉBALLAGE MARCH
MARCHÉ SAINT-PIERR
SAINT PIERRE
COUPONS MARCHE SA
LES TISSUS REIN
14

# Marché Saint-Pierre

At the bottom of the Montmartre hill around the Halle Saint-Pierre, Rue Charles Nodier, Rue d'Orsel, Rue Ronsard and Rue Livingstone, is the largest fabric market in the capital. The two biggest stores are **TISSUS REINE** and **DREYFUS**. They deal in mass-produced fabrics for clothing and furnishings. The selection is vast and inexpensive and you can also find all the accessories you need for sewing and embroidery. Smaller stores orbit around these two main ones—remnant sellers, specialists in leather, Liberty prints or tulle. Visit **SACRÉS COUPONS**, where you can find *Bonpoint* and *Claudie Pierlot* fabrics at attractive prices.

TISSUS REINE: 3–5 PLACE SAINT-PIERRE . 75018 . 01 46 06 02 31 . TISSUS-REINE.COM

DREYFUS: 2 RUE CHARLES NODIER . 75018 . 01 46 06 92 25

SACRÉS COUPONS : 4 BIS RUE D'ORSEL . 75018 . 01 42 64 69 96

MARCHESAINTPIERRE.COM . MÉTRO ANVERS

18th
Map p.278

# 03

## NATURE & BOTANICALS

Some things engage us through our senses. A haunting fragrance, the brush of a feather, a sumptuous colour, a gritty texture, the solitude of a garden—each evokes a tangible memory or perhaps merely a fleeting suggestion. The following places will appeal to your sensual side. It's only natural.

Gnarled wood • floral extracts • branches in bloom • pure essences • shells from faraway places • multicoloured feathers • inspiration • resins • floral boutiques • jasmine • shimmering hues • perfect refuge • jewel scarab • hedonism • amber • textured papers • ochres • subtle scents • medieval elixirs

72

# Parks & Gardens

Here are the main parks and gardens in Paris, and the metro stations closest to them. These havens are great for picnicking, playing sport, reading a book or just enjoying the peace and quiet of nature. Many other smaller spaces are hidden throughout the city; here are my favourites.

MONCEAU

Ⓜ

**PARC MONCEAU**

**BOIS DE BOULOGNE**

CHAMP-DE-MARS
TOUR EIFFEL

Ⓜ

**ESPLANADE DE
INVALIDES**

**CHAMP-DE-MARS**

PORTE D'AUTEUIL

Ⓜ

Ⓜ

**PARC ANDRÉ CITROËN**

To admire the charms of a French formal garden, with flower beds designed by André Le Nôtre in the seventeenth century, visit the **JARDIN DU LUXEMBOURG** and the **JARDIN DES TUILERIES**. The **JARDIN DES TUILERIES BOOKSTORE**, near the main gate to the garden, has some 4000 books on gardens and gardening. The **MUSÉE CARNAVALET** and the superb **BIBLIOTHÈQUE FORNEY**, specialising in the decorative and fine arts, also have small French-style gardens.

The **JARDIN DES PLANTES** in the south of Paris is the capital's main botanical garden. It covers 23.5 hectares and includes a small zoo, the superb Grande Galerie d'Évolution, a botany school, an alpine garden with shrubs and herbaceous plants from mountainous environments around the world, a rose garden and four large greenhouses (Mexican, Australian, New Caledonian and the winter garden).

**JARDIN SAINT-GILLES-GRAND-VENEUR** in the 3rd arrondissement is a wonderful surprise. It's not easy to find because it's hidden among small streets at the intersection of Rue de Hesse and Rue du Grand Veneur, near Boulevard Beaumarchais. It's a small garden that is especially charming, particularly in early summer as it contains a rose garden. The ideal place for a break.

**PARC DE SCEAUX**

 PARC DE SCEAUX

If you're in the 5th arrondissement, take a look at the **ARÈNES DE LUTÈCE**, built in the third century AD. It's quite amazing and the ultimate spot for a game of pétanque.

The **MUSÉE DE LA VIE ROMANTIQUE** is also a pleasant spot to escape the bustle of Paris. You can have lunch there or a cup of tea.

The garden of the **HÔTEL PARTICULIER MONTMARTRE** is the perfect refuge for lunch or a drink in summer.

Just outside Paris, the **PARC DE SCEAUX** dazzles visitors every year in April with the flowering of about 250 cherry trees. It's ideal for celebrating Hanami, the Japanese cherry blossom festival.

# Stéphane Chapelle

The term 'florist' doesn't do it justice. The gold-painted walls of this store show the patina of time and provide an elegant setting for a refined selection. Outside, a forest of shrubs and greenery invites you to slow down. Inside are branches of cherry and pear blossom and hydrangeas. Stéphane Chapelle goes to Rungis market every morning to fill last-minute orders and source the best for his customers.

29 RUE DE RICHELIEU . 75001 . 01 42 60 65 66
MÉTRO PALAIS ROYAL–MUSÉE DU LOUVRE

1st
Map p. 260

*The street is full of Japanese shops and you are quite close to a number of good restaurants. **Kunitoraya** has the best udon noodles in Paris and **Izakaya Issé** offers an excellent €13 set menu. A little further along, Nicolas will be delighted to receive you at **Télescope** café.*

# Hervé Châtelain

Immaculate presentation is the secret of Hervé Châtelain. Both the display window and store are superb and it feels like you are discovering each flower anew. There are hydrangeas, roses, lilies—all the usual suspects. But what makes this florist exceptional is the special care given to the arrangement of colours and blooms. You can also find the lovely *Pan Puri* and *Rigaud* scented candles.

140 RUE MONTMARTRE . 75002 . 01 45 08 85 57

MÉTRO BOURSE

2nd

*Map p. 262*

If you're ready for a meal, consider **Coinstot Vino** and **Racines** restaurants, or the very good but more expensive **Passage 53**, all in the nearby Passage des Panoramas. You're also close to two of the best bistros in Paris: **Le Gavroche**, which doesn't look like much from the outside, and **Aux Lyonnais**.

# *Odorantes*

Close to the Église Saint-Sulpice, *Odorantes* is a chic floral boutique where fragrance rules. It's well known to the fashion world, working with some of the finest Parisian couture houses. The House of Chanel, for example, orders black roses here, dyed using a special absorption method.

9 RUE MADAME . 75006 . 01 42 84 03 00 . ODORANTES-PARIS.COM
MÉTRO SAINT-SULPICE

*6th*
*Map p.268*

# Flower

You can spot the entrance to *Flower* on Rue des Saints-Pères from quite a distance: flowers invade the footpath and it's hard to know which way to turn once you step inside. Cécile is the talent behind this shop. She works with blooms of exceptional quality and decorates many Parisian terraces and gardens. The walls of red fabric form a backdrop for an artwork of fragrant roses, dahlias, autumn hydrangeas and branches that extends from floor to ceiling. A second store with a garden workshop vibe has opened a few steps away in Rue de Babylone.

14 RUE DES SAINTS-PÈRES . 75007 . 01 44 50 00 20 . FLOWER.FR
MÉTRO ST-GERMAIN-DES-PRÉS

*7th*
Map p.270

*To grab a quick lunch or buy some gourmet provisions, head towards Rue de Verneuil.* **L'Épicerie Générale** *makes delicious sandwiches, salads and fresh fruit juices. If you fancy a sit-down lunch or dinner, try the* **Cinq-Mars** *restaurant further along the street. For dinner, however, it's best to make a reservation.*

# Les Mauvaises Graines

They don't call themselves florists at *Les Mauvaises Graines*, they're 'plantists'. Tucked away in the north of the 18th arrondissement, the store has a resolutely different look. Fake grass on the floor and no cut flowers. Instead there are plants, pretty antiques and vintage objects, a little taxidermy and a lot of passion for the offbeat and rock'n'roll. Larkspurs, delphiniums, lupins, bronze fennel ... everything here is natural and pesticide-free. Also, *Les Mauvaises Graines* will happily reorganise and decorate your patio, garden or balcony.

25 RUE CUSTINE . 75018 . 01 55 79 71 35 . LESMAUVAISESGRAINES.COM
MÉTRO CHÂTEAU ROUGE

18th
Map p. 278

*Opposite* **Les Mauvaises Graines** *you'll find* **Les Peintures XVIIIième**, *with its beautiful selection of paints and wallpapers.*

# Claude Nature

After spending several years at **DEYROLLE**, Claude opened his own shop on Boulevard Saint-Germain, specialising in insects, shells, birds and butterflies. At number 32 you'll find all kinds of amazing—yet quite affordable—specimens from around the world. Jewel scarabs from Costa Rica in gold, green, blue and red. Deep green rainbow stag beetles from Australia or incredible leaf insects from Indonesia. You can also buy entomology equipment here. You'll receive a friendly welcome and come away with lots of interesting and surprising information. Did you know, for example, that the horseshoe crab has existed in the same form for 500 million years and is used every day for medical purposes? Each visit becomes a short course in natural science.

32 BOULEVARD SAINT-GERMAIN . 75005 . 01 44 07 30 79 . CLAUDENATURE.COM
MÉTRO MAUBERT-MUTUALITÉ

5*th*

# Deyrolle

A Parisian institution since 1831, this is the shop no lover of taxidermy can miss. Thankfully, the site has recovered from a terrible fire in February 2008. The store is now more beautiful than ever and has just launched a magnificent collection of wallpaper inspired by its educational posters.

There are two other Parisian stores specialising in taxidermy: **GALERIE CHARDON**, at 21–23 Rue des Filles du Calvaire and **DESIGN ET NATURE**, in Rue d'Aboukir.

46 RUE DU BAC . 75007 . 01 42 22 30 07 . DEYROLLE.FR

MÉTRO RUE DU BAC

7th
Map p. 270

# Hermès

The *Hermès* store in Rue de Sèvres occupies a former swimming pool that once belonged to the Hotel Lutétia. Much of the original architecture has been preserved. What was once the bottom of the pool is now covered with mosaics, the shimmering turquoise and azure shades evoking the water. Two wooden huts showcase the craftsmanship that is a hallmark of the *Hermès* brand. For sheer spatial design and beauty, you can't go past this store. You will also find *Hermès* tableware, jewellery, furniture and wallpaper here, as well as magnificent saddles and equestrian accessories monogrammed with the famous 'H'. Discover, also, the *Petit H* collections, one-off items created from scraps of leather, fabric, glass or wood. A famous *Hermès* scarf becomes a ship's sail, while the leather off-cuts of a *Kelly* bag cover wooden stools. Dive in and enjoy!

17 RUE DE SÈVRES . 75006 . 01 42 22 80 83 . HERMES.COM
MÉTRO SÈVRES-BABYLONE

*6th*
*Map p. 268*

**La Maison du Chocolat** *is next door, selling excellent truffles and other chocolate treats.* **Le Bon Marché**, *the city's most chic department store, and* **La Grande Épicerie de Paris** *are a five-minute walk away along Rue de Sèvres, at numbers 24 and 38 respectively.*

# Odeur de Sainteté

I first saw these pretty bottles, with their divine, sometimes dark and always lyrical names, at **ASTIER DE VILLATTE**. Chantal Sanier is the alchemist behind this beautiful creation. In her skilled hands, perfume takes on a special dimension, rich and full of character. The scent emerges and, like a living organism, evolves on the individual wearer. The descriptions on the bottles are elegant and poetic. These 'supernatural perfumes', as Chantal likes to call them, have medieval connotations and are blended without preservatives. You will discover nine elixirs at *Astier de Villatte* and **MERCI**. You can also contact Chantal Sanier direct; if you're lucky, she may let you into her magnificent studio at Quai du Louvre.

BY APPOINTMENT ONLY . 22 QUAI DU LOUVRE . 75001 . 01 42 21 38 33

ODEURDESAINTETE.COM . MÉTRO PONT NEUF

1st
Map p. 260

# Miller et Bertaux

This store is somewhat difficult to classify. It is above all a place of inspiration. You'll find wonderful little objects from different places. Wrapping paper from Morocco, *Antonia Rossi*'s woven dolls, superb ceramics, handmade fabrics from Bali and pretty candles. The selection is always classy, as is the choice of materials and colours. The fact that there are no brand names, just objects that are almost one-offs, makes this one of my favourite addresses in Paris.

17 RUE FERDINAND DUVAL . 75004 . 01 42 78 28 39 . MILLERETBERTAUX.COM
MÉTRO SAINT-PAUL

4<sup>th</sup>
Map p. 266

*If you get peckish, head to Rue des Rosiers.* **L'As du Fallafel**, *at number 34, makes one of the best falafels in Paris. Enjoy the best of Ashkenazi cuisine at number 27, with pastrami sandwiches, superb cheesecake and apfel strudel from* **Sacha Finkelsztajn (La boutique jaune)**; *or try* **Florence Kahn** *at 24 Rue des Écouffes.*

# Mad et Len at l'Éclaireur

**L'ÉCLAIREUR** is recognised worldwide for unearthing new and avant-garde talent. The store at 10 Rue Herold is a particularly grand and luxurious space. You'll find magnificent rugs from the Danish brand *Private 0204* here. The wonderfully fragrant *Mad et Len* products, which I first discovered at the Tranoï trade show, are available from the *l'Éclaireur* shop in Rue Malher in the Marais. Their scented candles, manufactured in the south of France and presented in heavy, round black boxes, have a look that's decidedly beautiful, austere, dark and elegant.

10 RUE HEROLD . 75001 . MÉTRO ÉTIENNE MARCEL
12 RUE MALHER . 75004 . MÉTRO SAINT-PAUL
SEE LECLAIREUR.COM FOR OTHER ADDRESSES

1st
*Map p. 260*

# Diptyque

The store that saw the birth of the *Diptyque* brand more than fifty years ago has retained the history of its founding trio. Although the brand is now synonymous with perfume, the first *Diptyque* creations were fabric and wallpaper designs. Located at 34 Boulevard Saint-Germain, the flagship store displays the wallpapers they created for *Liberty* and *Sanderson* at the time. They successfully introduced perfumes from England, then decided to create their own. The rest is history.

34 BOULEVARD SAINT-GERMAIN . 75005 . 01 43 26 77 44 . DIPTYQUEPARIS.FR

MÉTRO MAUBERT-MUTUALITÉ

5*th*

*For lunch in the area,* **La Crèmerie,** *a bistro and wine bar at 9 rue des Quatre-Vents, serves simple yet delicious fare, including possibly the best burrata in Paris.* LACREMERIE.FR

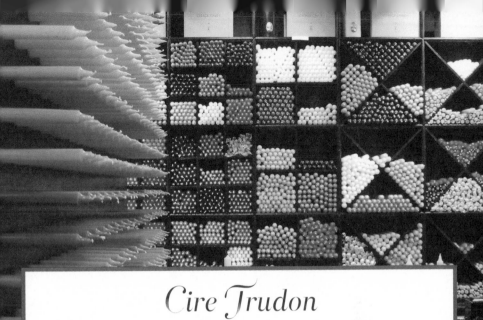

# Cire Trudon

*Cire Trudon* has played a part in the history of the French monarchy since 1643, first as a supplier of wax to Versailles, then as a candlemaker for Napoléon. The house of Trudon has managed to survive all those years and remains a benchmark for scented candles around the world. At *Cire Trudon* you'll find their iconic scented candles, pillar candles with cameos and a huge variety of candle colours. *Cire Trudon* has also revived the 'stink bomb'—tiny throw-down vials of scent, which fortunately release an exquisite perfume.

78 RUE DE SEINE . 75006 . 01 43 26 46 50 . CIRETRUDON.COM
MÉTRO ODÉON

*6ᵗʰ*
Map p. 268

*Nearby, there are several lovely stores along the Rue Saint-Sulpice and Rue des Quatre-Vents.* **Catherine Memmi** *sells beautiful ceramics by* **Christiane Perrochon** *and* **Secret Maison** *has gorgeous household linens.*

# The quais & flower market

Apart from the traditional florists, there are two other noteworthy places in Paris dedicated to flowers and plants. Located beside the river at Quai de la Mégisserie is **VILMORIN**. This is the place to come for all your indoor and outdoor plants, seeds, pots, potting soil and gardening equipment.

**MARCHÉ AUX FLEURS ET AUX OISEAUX**—the flower and bird market—on the Île de la Cité is open every day from 8 am to 7 pm, offering flowers and plants. On Sunday it becomes the bird market, selling a wide variety of birds, seeds and cages. If you're interested in herbalism, visit the **HERBORISTERIE DU PALAIS-ROYAL**.

MARCHÉ AUX FLEURS ET AUX OISEAUX: PLACE LOUIS LÉPINE & QUAI DE LA CORSE . 75004 . MÉTRO CITÉ
VILMORIN: QUAI DE LA MÉGISSERIE . 75001 . MÉTRO CHÂTELET

1st . 4th
Map p. 260
– p. 266

# 04

## ART & COLOUR

A deft hand, a gift for colour, a mastery of technique developed through practice, a driving passion—these are the hallmarks of the treasured artisans of Paris. Come and meet a few of the craftsmen and craftswomen I've been fortunate enough to encounter and discover some of Paris' finest art supplies stores. Who knows, you might even be inspired to explore your own creative talents.

Paintbrushes • Kozo Usukuchi paper • a solid oilstick in Flemish blue • vials of resin • ink blots on fabric • engraved paper • canvases • pastel powders tracing a contour • the smell of varnish • a creaking parquet floor

3111 Rouge Gera
3211 Rouge Cap
3931 Rouge de

3361 Soleil coll
3421 Ocre Roug
3441 Ocre dore

3541 Ocre d'Or
3611 Vermillon de Chine
3631 Vermillon de Cadmium

de Cadmium X
brillant

3831 Carmin brûle
3911 Rouge au Ja
4111 Jaune Souc

# La Maison du Pastel

A must for all lovers of colour, *La Maison du Pastel* has been given a new lease on life by Isabelle Roché. Descended from a long line of pastel manufacturers, she has taken up the torch in brilliant style by learning the secrets of producing these little sticks of colour. It's exciting to listen to Isabelle talk about her passion and the history of the company. The colours are so magnificent you just know you'll be able to create a masterpiece with them.

20 RUE RAMBUTEAU . 75003 . 01 40 29 00 67 . LAMAISONDUPASTEL.COM
OPEN THURSDAY AFTERNOONS OR BY APPOINTMENT . MÉTRO RAMBUTEAU

4<sup>th</sup>
*Map p. 266*

*You are only two minutes from the delicious* **Pain de Sucre** *pâtisserie at 14 Rue Rambuteau,* 01 45 74 68 92 . PATISSERIEPAINDESUCRE.COM

# *Calligrane*

*Calligrane* is in Rue du Pont Louis-Philippe, the 'paper' street, close to the river and not far from the bustling department store **BAZAR DE L'HÔTEL DE VILLE (BHV)**. Over time the street has come to specialise in paper, attracting establishments with different styles, including **PAPIER PLUS**, **MÉLODIES GRAPHIQUES** and **CALLIGRANE**. *Calligrane* is aimed at designers, photographers and lovers of beautiful materials. Specialising in Japanese paper, they sell elegant handmade papers in different sizes and textures—works of art in themselves. There are papers made from fruits and vegetables, Mayan papers, papers from Bhutan, Thailand and Brazil—more than a hundred kinds. The papers have also been made into notebooks by young artists. You can have business cards created here and certain kinds of binding done. There is also beautiful stationery, small leather goods and other paper-based objects.

6 RUE DU PONT LOUIS-PHILIPPE . 75004 . 01 48 04 09 00 . CALLIGRANE.FR

MÉTRO PONT MARIE

4ᵗʰ
*Map p. 266*

# Papier Plus

This store has been in existence since 1976 and sells a wide range of notebooks, photo albums and presentation boxes. Each line is designed by *Papier Plus* and made by French artisans. The finish and quality of the papers used produces a high-end product. Some customers, designers and writers have been returning for more than ten years, often buying the same notebook in the same format and colour and filling them with notes and drafts to keep as memoirs. One regular patron bought his 260th volume this year. Now, that's noteworthy.

9 RUE DU PONT LOUIS-PHILIPPE . 75004 . 01 42 77 70 49
PAPIERPLUS.COM . MÉTRO PONT MARIE

4th
Map p. 266

# Lavrut

*Lavrut* has been in Passage Choiseul since 1922, the store passed down from father to son. Over the years the company has branched out into several specialist areas—a stationery store with an interesting collection of little notebooks, a printing house and an art supplies store. Joining forces with the longstanding **ADAM** store at 11 Boulevard Edgar Quinet in the 14th arrondissement, the two establishments now carry on the expertise and traditions of Paris' older art supplies stores.

52 PASSAGE CHOISEUL . 75002 . 01 42 96 95 54 . ADAM-LAVRUT.COM
MÉTRO QUATRE-SEPTEMBRE
ADAM MONTPARNASSE : 11 BD EDGAR QUINET . 75014
01 43 20 68 53 . MÉTRO EDGAR QUINET

2nd
Map p. 262

*Lavrut*
*depuis 1922*

# Benneton

The *Benneton* engraving house has been in business since 1880. It boasts many loyal customers from the worlds of fashion and politics, and individuals with a taste for beauty. *Benneton* has mastered the traditional technique of brushed stamping, its craftspeople—members of the professional artisan association Meilleurs Ouvriers de France—achieving impeccable quality and excellence. Each note card is decorated with hand-applied gouache borders, giving soul to a precious and personal piece of correspondence.

If you are keen to try engraving, **CHARBONNEL** has all the equipment you'll need.

75 BOULEVARD MALESHERBES . 75008 . 01 43 87 57 39
BOUTIQUE.BENNETONGRAVEUR.COM . MÉTRO SAINT-AUGUSTIN
CHARBONNEL: 13 QUAI MONTEBELLO . 75005
01 43 54 23 46 . MÉTRO PLACE SAINT-MICHEL

*8th*

# *Sennelier*

Established 125 years ago, this store presides over three floors, presenting a mixture of incredible watercolour charts, painting knives, brushes, pigments, glass mullers for grinding pigments in wooden cases, inks, oils, Schira porcelain paints and notepads. It's well known for the oils and watercolours developed by Gustave Sennelier, which have served as inspiration for many painters, such as Cézanne and Picasso. A special feature of this store is its 'papers of the world' department on the top floor. The department manager is passionate about his subject and has worked in the field for forty years. You will find all kinds of paper here—Japanese, Korean, Indian and even amate paper made from bark, used by the Aztecs. I also find beautiful notebooks here, like the ones from **LA COMPAGNIE DU KRAFT**, whose shop is in Rue Jacob in the 6th arrondissement (LEKRAFT.COM).

LES COULEURS DU QUAI . 3 QUAI VOLTAIRE . 75007 . 01 42 60 72 15
MAGASINSENNELIER.COM . MÉTRO PALAIS ROYAL–MUSÉE DU LOUVRE

7th
*Map p. 270*

*The magnificent campus of **École des Beaux-Arts de Paris**—the school of fine arts—is close by in Rue Bonaparte. If the gate is open, feel free to go in and look around.*

# Dubois

Located in the beautiful student quarter around the **PANTHÉON**, a few steps from the **JARDIN DU LUXEMBOURG**, *Dubois*, originally a paint manufacturer, is one of those old Parisian institutions that has stayed in the same family. The store retains its 1861 style, with lots of wooden drawers and the original floor. You'll find all fine arts supplies here—even small wooden artist's models that are fully articulated, including hands, knees and pelvis.

20 RUE SOUFFLOT . 75005 . 01 44 41 67 50
DUBOIS-PARIS.COM . MÉTRO CLUNY–LA SORBONNE

5*th*

# Laverdure & Fils

I was given this address by a sculptor when I was looking for objects for a piece on Rome. In a street a little set back from the bustle of Boulevard du Faubourg Saint-Antoine, *Laverdure* looks like it has been here forever. You will find all the supplies you need for sculpting and framing.

58 RUE TRAVERSIÈRE . 75012 . 01 43 43 38 85 . LAVERDURE.FR
MÉTRO LEDRU-ROLLIN

12<sup>th</sup>

# Cristalleries Schweitzer

From the outside you can already hear the sanders at work. This Parisian workshop, the workplace of three young artisans (all girls!) who are carrying on the tradition of the company, is undoubtedly unique. *Cristalleries Schweitzer* repairs and restores all kinds of glass. It's the place to go when a glass from an old set is chipped or the stopper of a carafe is cracked.

84 QUAI DE JEMMAPES . 75010 . 01 42 39 61 63 . CRISTALLERIES-SCHWEITZER.FR
MÉTRO JACQUES BONSERGENT

*10th*
Map p. 274

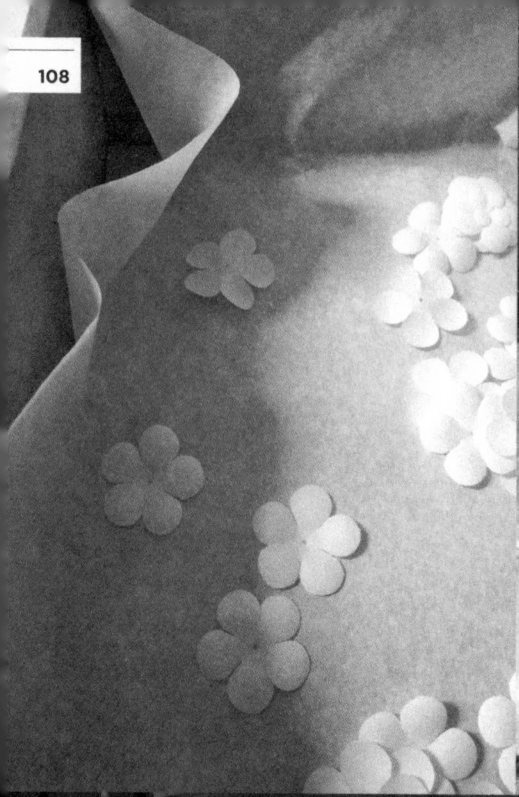

LEGERON

*Fleurs et Plumes*

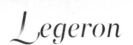

# Legeron

*Legeron* is one of those classic old Parisian workshops that still operates today. Inside a courtyard on the lively Rue des Petits Champs, the house of *Legeron* has worked on various haute couture commissions and collections since 1880. Nimble hands busily cut, shape, dye and assemble real feathers and fake flowers to adorn the creations of the greatest couturiers—jackets, dresses and hats. They use vintage tools and machines and the techniques they employ display a perfect mastery and knowledge of their trade. *Legeron*'s expertise and the creations they produce are awe-inspiring. You can have a piece custom-made for a wedding or special occasion. It's best to call ahead to make an appointment, rather than simply drop in unannounced.

To help create your own masterpiece, you can buy feathers from **RD SPECTACLES** in the 2nd arrondissement.

20 RUE DES PETITS CHAMPS . 75002 . 01 42 96 94 89 . LEGERON.COM . MÉTRO OPÉRA
RD SPECTACLES: 82 RUE DE CLÉRY . 75002 . 01 40 26 71 86 . RD-SPECTACLES.FR
MÉTRO STRASBOURG-SAINT-DENIS

2nd
Map p. 262

# Cuirs Chadefaux

*Chadefaux* supplies leather to some of the great Parisian upholstery houses, such as *Lelièvre*. Vegetable tanning results in a high-quality product that's much sought after for leather goods, saddlery and upholstery. You'll also find leatherworking tools and reels of leather laces in different colours.

18 RUE TAYLOR . 75010 . 01 42 08 18 61 . CUIRSCHADEFAUX.COM
MÉTRO JACQUES BONSERGENT

*10th*
*Map p.274*

BEURRE 942

SOLEIL 700

# Peausserie Poulain

The house of *Poulain* provides soft leathers to haute couture and interior decorating clients. It has been offering different types of leather, such as suede goatskin and lambskin, available in multiple colours, since 1919.

52 BOULEVARD RICHARD LENOIR . 75011 . 01 48 05 54 54 . PEAUSSERIEPOULAIN.COM
MÉTRO RICHARD-LENOIR

**11**th
Map p.276

# Patricia Vieljeux

There's a lot going on along Rue Godefroy Cavaignac. At number 21 is the workshop of ceramist Patricia Vieljeux, who sells beautiful turned pieces in stoneware and porcelain. I go there in particular for her cups. You can also take courses there.

21 RUE GODEFROY CAVAIGNAC . 75011 . 01 46 59 04 10 . PATRICIAVIELJEUX.COM
MÉTRO VOLTAIRE OR CHARONNE

11<sup>th</sup>
*Map p. 276*

**BAR A MANGER**

Olives De Sicile Marinées
Guindillas Poêlées A La Fleur De Sel
Radis "Red Meat" Noisettes Caille De Chene
Anchois De Cantabrie
Bonite Fumée Au Bois De Pommier...
...Chou Rave Pomme
Boquerones Fenouil Grillé
Carpaccio De Mulet Noir Creme Cru...
Poutargue
Huitre "Roumegous" N°4 Au BBQ x1=3
Huitre "Utah Beach" 3 x1=3/x6=17/x12=3
Saucisson Sec De Porc Noir
Magret De Canard Fumé Maison
Chorizo De Porc Noir
Jambon De Bigorre
Assiette De Fromages
Sorbet De Peche Maison Champagne

Still on Rue Godefroy Cavaignac, at number 43, is **Bones**, the restaurant of young Australian chef James Henry. If you backtrack up the street, you'll come to the very good **Septime** and its new restaurant specialising in seafood at 80 Rue de Charonne. A little further along on the corner, at 3 Rue Basfroi, is the wine bar **Septime La Cave**.

# Emmanuelle Wittmann

Emmanuelle Wittmann has a lovely studio, *Affinité Terre*, on Rue des Récollets in the 10th arrondissement. She works in porcelain and stoneware and also gives classes.

13 RUE DES RÉCOLLETS . 75010 . 01 43 80 01 24 . AFFINITE-TERRE.FR

MÉTRO CHÂTEAU LANDON

*10th*
Map p. 274

# Talents

*Talents* is the boutique of the Ateliers d'Arts de France association, which represents ceramists and artists from every corner of France. I go there for the creations of *Nathalie Audibert*, plates from *Faïencerie Georges* and vases by *Simone Perrotte*.

1 BIS RUE SCRIBE . 75009 . 01 40 17 98 38 . BOUTIQUESTALENTS.COM
MÉTRO OPÉRA

9th
Map p. 272

# 05

## TOOL BOX

Some places selling tools and equipment have been in the game for many years—remaining in all their original, unadulterated glory—and are really worth a visit. These stores are specialists, often in business for generation after generation, selling items that may be impossible to find elsewhere. Dispensing specialist knowledge and distributing quality products are their tools of trade.

Chain mail ⬡

wood glue ⬡ restoration

⬡ matte and powdered

paints ⬡ gold plating ⬡

pulleys and straps ⬡ stone

fireplace ⬡ wire mesh ⬡

dowels ⬡ wood-screws ⬡

sandpaper ⬡ bronze locks

⬡ stone basin ⬡ paint

and lacquer ⬡ zelliges ⬡

plaster and concrete

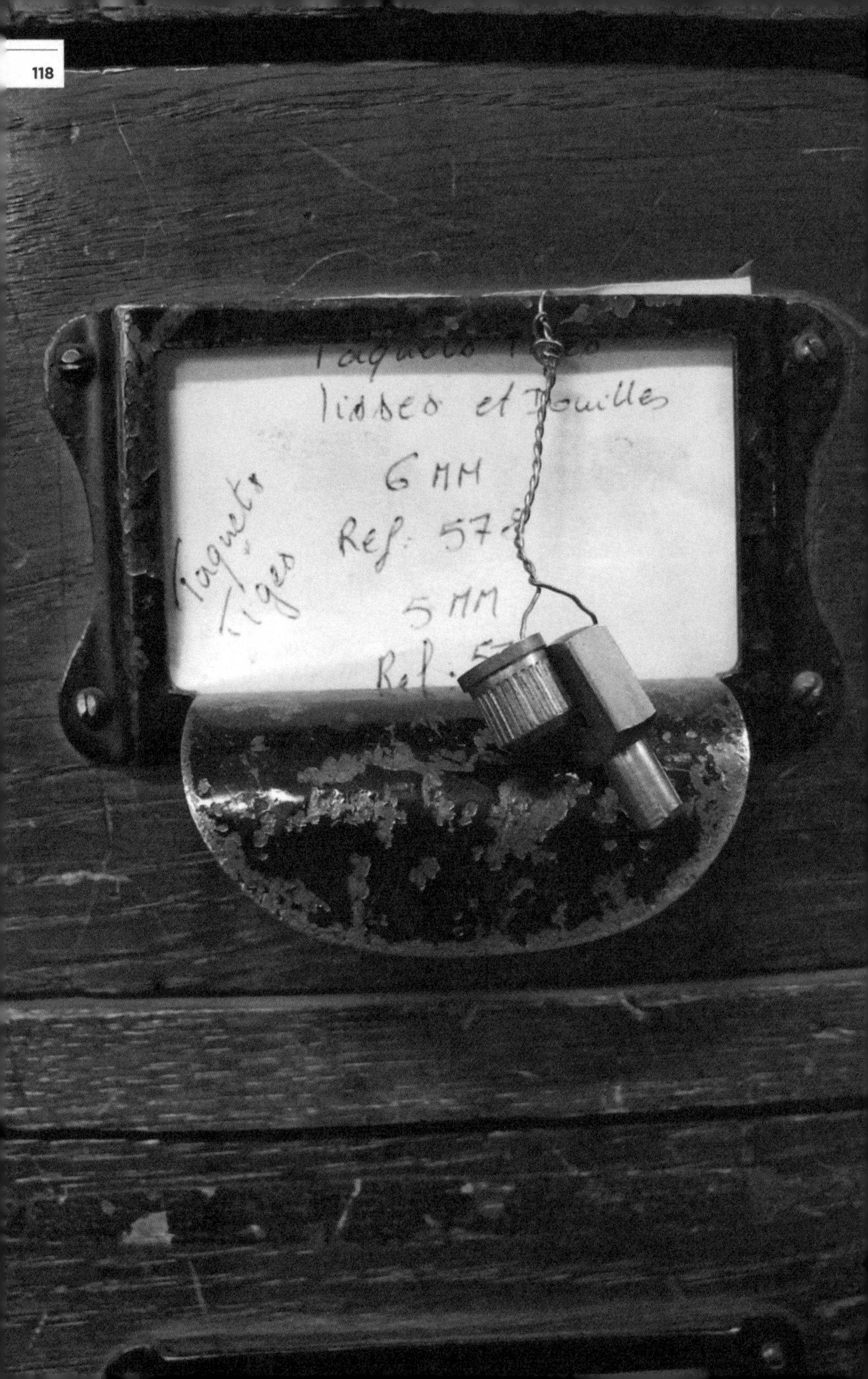
lisses et Douilles
6 MM
5 MM
Paquets
Tiges

TUBES LAITON
DISPONIBLES

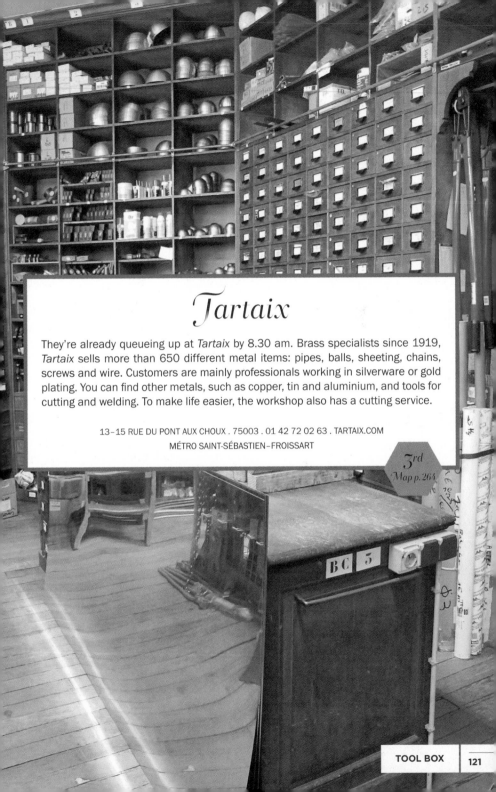

# Tartaix

They're already queueing up at *Tartaix* by 8.30 am. Brass specialists since 1919, *Tartaix* sells more than 650 different metal items: pipes, balls, sheeting, chains, screws and wire. Customers are mainly professionals working in silverware or gold plating. You can find other metals, such as copper, tin and aluminium, and tools for cutting and welding. To make life easier, the workshop also has a cutting service.

13–15 RUE DU PONT AUX CHOUX . 75003 . 01 42 72 02 63 . TARTAIX.COM
MÉTRO SAINT-SÉBASTIEN–FROISSART

3rd
Map p.264

Lunettes
de sécurité
obligatoires

Gants
de sécurité
obligatoires

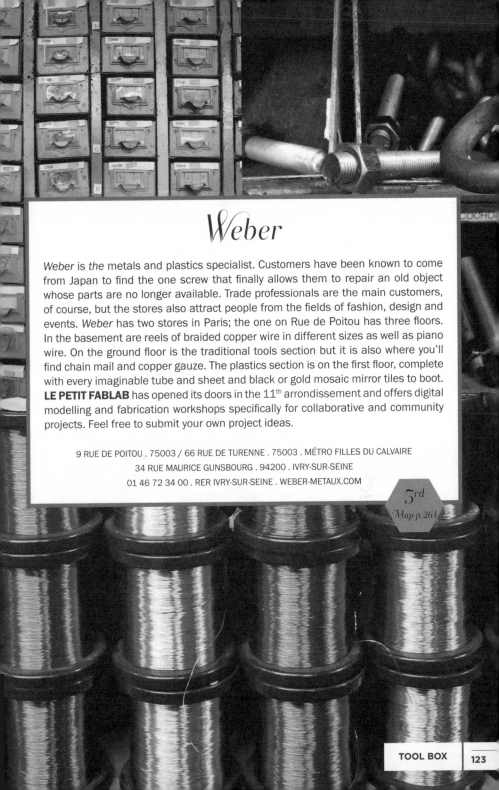

# Weber

*Weber* is *the* metals and plastics specialist. Customers have been known to come from Japan to find the one screw that finally allows them to repair an old object whose parts are no longer available. Trade professionals are the main customers, of course, but the stores also attract people from the fields of fashion, design and events. *Weber* has two stores in Paris; the one on Rue de Poitou has three floors. In the basement are reels of braided copper wire in different sizes as well as piano wire. On the ground floor is the traditional tools section but it is also where you'll find chain mail and copper gauze. The plastics section is on the first floor, complete with every imaginable tube and sheet and black or gold mosaic mirror tiles to boot. **LE PETIT FABLAB** has opened its doors in the 11th arrondissement and offers digital modelling and fabrication workshops specifically for collaborative and community projects. Feel free to submit your own project ideas.

9 RUE DE POITOU . 75003 / 66 RUE DE TURENNE . 75003 . MÉTRO FILLES DU CALVAIRE
34 RUE MAURICE GUNSBOURG . 94200 . IVRY-SUR-SEINE
01 46 72 34 00 . RER IVRY-SUR-SEINE . WEBER-METAUX.COM

*3rd*
*Map p.264*

# Au Progrès

This magical hardware store has hardly changed since 1873. It is filled with old oak drawers and the original cash register is still there. Specialising in bronze and iron, *Au Progrès* offers a wide selection of Empire-style, Louis XIV-style and Louis XV-style locks. They're sure to have just what you're looking for. The clever people at *Au Progrès* can also remake bronze parts to your specifications. If you get the chance, ask to visit the workshop upstairs—it's magic.

11 BIS RUE FAIDHERBE CHALIGNY . 75011 . 01 43 71 70 61 . AUPROGRES.COM
MÉTRO FAIDHERBE CHALIGNY

**11ᵗʰ**
*Map p. 276*

*This neighbourhood has preserved some of the old artisanal trades, including blacksmithing and cabinetmaking. For coffee, lunch or dinner, head to Rue Paul Bert. There's a charming café with a terrace, **Le Pure Café**, at 14 Rue Jean Macé; **Bistrot Paul Bert** at 18 Rue Paul Bert; **L'Écailler du Bistrot** at 22 Rue Paul Bert; and right next door at number 24, **La Pâtisserie Cyril Lignac** has a delicious baba au rhum and an incredible kouign-amann.*

PLATE 45    PLATE 50    PLATE 55

PLATE 110    PLATE 125    PLATE 145

T. HOMME 45    T. HOMME 50    T. HOMME 55

12    15    18

TÊTES RONDES 4 PANS

16/25    16/45    18/50

TÊTES POINTE DIAMANT HAUTE

# Le Comptoir Alexandre

This is the light bulb specialist. A tiny shop filled with cardboard boxes and myriad models in every style. You can also find bulbs for light therapy, to help get you through a depressing winter, and compact fluorescent bulbs for plants.

58 RUE DE PARADIS . 75010 . 01 48 24 67 36
COMPTOIRALEXANDRE.COM . MÉTRO CADET

10th
Map p.274

# À l' Épi d' Or

Next to the Bernardine convent, in a little street leading to the Boulevard Saint-Germain, is the showroom of *À l'Épi d'Or*, a bathrooms specialist since the early twentieth century. The products are created by French artisans. You'll find loads of taps, standing mirrors, soap dishes, stone basins and pedestal sinks in an Art Deco style. They also have some older pieces, such as an antique dressing table.

17 RUE DES BERNARDINS . 75005 . 01 46 33 17 16
SALLEDEBAIN-EPIDOR.COM . MÉTRO MAUBERT-MUTUALITÉ

*5ᵗʰ*

# Emery & Cie

This store is in the Passage de la Main d'Or in the 11th arrondissement, not far from the **MARCHÉ D'ALIGRE**. It's a Belgian company. I go there specifically for their cement tiles and zelliges. They have their own beautiful and extensive line of paints and lacquers, and pretty little ceramic bowls in these shades.

18 PASSAGE DE LA MAIN D'OR . 75011 . 01 44 87 02 02 . EMERYETCIE.COM
MÉTRO LEDRU-ROLLIN

11th
Map p. 276

23.    22.    21.    20.    18.

30.    31.    32.    33.    34.    35.

# The Little Shop of Colours

This little shop sells a wide range of paints in divine colours, plus rust-effect paints, waxed concrete and a collection of fluorescent paints. It has also brought wallpaper-effect painting back into fashion by developing a stamp roller technique.

1 RUE DE JARENTE . 75004 . 01 42 71 36 75 . TLSPARIS.COM
MÉTRO SAINT-PAUL

4<sup>th</sup>
Map p. 266

# Mise en Teinte

*Mise en Teinte*'s two Paris stores sell top brand names for painting and decorating, including paints such as the *Flamant* and *Farrow and Ball* ranges, as well as *Tollens*, which collaborated with *Mise en Teinte* to create the *Mise en Teinte–Édition Tollens* range. There are also natural fibre and cork floor coverings, carpets and wallpapers from *Cole & Son*, *Nina Campbell* and *Osborne and Little*. This is an excellent establishment offering a quality range.

15 BOULEVARD SAINT-GERMAIN . 75005 . 01 46 34 44 58 . MÉTRO MAUBERT-MUTUALITÉ

44 AVENUE VICTOR HUGO . 75016 . 01 45 00 03 20 . MÉTRO KLÉBER

MISEENTEINTE.COM

5th · 16th

# Carrelages des Suds

A top-shelf selection of floorings: stone slabs from Burgundy, Southern Europe and Italy, textured marbles and enamelled terracotta from Spain. The tiles are for the most part produced by traditional artisanal methods.

24 BOULEVARD SAINT-GERMAIN . 75005 . 01 40 51 01 01

MÉTRO MAUBERT-MUTUALITÉ

5ᵗʰ

# $\mathcal{R}$essource

*Ressource* regularly creates new paint collections in collaboration with influential figures from the decorating world, in accordance with its goal to work in the spirit of the great fabric and wallpaper producers. The paints are manufactured in France following a long tradition of respect for the environment. The collections offer multiple options—vivid colours designed with *Serge Bensimon*, shades of the 1950s with *Patrick Baty*, a wide range of off-whites, a beautiful line of effect paints, including brushed and Venetian-style plasters, and patinas for furniture.

62 RUE LA BOÉTIE . 75008 . 01 45 61 38 05 . MÉTRO MIROMESNIL
2–4 AVENUE DU MAINE . 75015 . 01 42 22 58 80 . MÉTRO GAÎTÉ
RESSOURCE-PEINTURES.COM

$8^{th}$ . $15^{th}$

# Mercadier

The *Mercadier* store has set itself up in the little Passage du Chantier. It specialises in waxed concrete, decorative coatings and natural clays. *Mercadier* offers close to seventy-two colours of concrete coatings and around fifty colours in different styles of poured concrete flooring.

16 PASSAGE DU CHANTIER . 75012 . 01 49 28 97 53 . PARIS.MERCADIER.FR
MÉTRO LEDRU-ROLLIN

*12ᵗʰ*

# Pierre & Vestiges

Here is a totally fantastic place. A massive warehouse in a former foundry just outside Paris, specialising in the restoration of cut stone pieces, particularly fireplaces. It's a presentation showroom and workshop in one, where masons, marble workers and fireplace specialists work to bring pieces from another time back to life.

26 RUE HENRI REGNAULT . 92150 SURESNES . 01 45 06 26 94
ANDREE-MACE.COM

## *Paris artisans who can help you:*

### RESTORE AN ANTIQUE MERCURY MIRROR

VINCENT GUERRE: 20 RUE CHAUCHAT . 75009 . 01 42 46 48 50

MIROIR-ANCIEN-VINCENT-GUERRE.COM . MÉTRO LE PELETIER

### RESTUFF OR RECANE A CHAIR

CANNAGE-PAILLAGE À L'ANCIENNE: 58 RUE DE CHARONNE . 75011

01 48 05 29 40 . MÉTRO LEDRU-ROLLIN

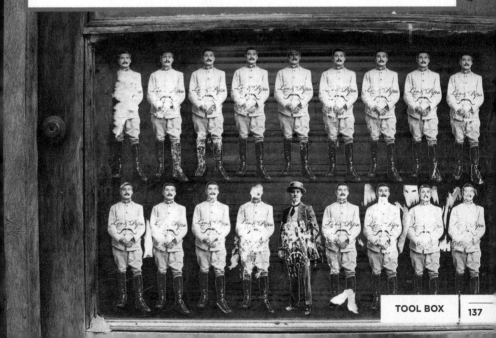

**MAKE OR RESTORE A BED BASE, MATTRESS, ARMCHAIR OR SOFA**

ATELIER GARNERO: 46 BOULEVARD BRUNE . 75014 . 01 45 43 70 08

ATELIERGARNERO.FR . MÉTRO MALAKOFF–PLATEAU DE VANVES

**REPAIR A COPPER SAUCEPAN, CASSEROLE OR JAM PAN**

L'ATELIER DU CUIVRE: 111 AVENUE DAUMESNIL . 75012 . 01 43 40 20 20

ATELIERARTSCULINAIRES.COM . MÉTRO REUILLY-DIDEROT

# 06

## VINTAGE

In the north of Paris is the *Puces de Saint-Ouen* flea market, the largest antiques market in the world. To the south, every weekend you can browse the smaller *Puces de Vanves* market. And throughout Paris there are numerous shops, second-hand markets, 'junk' sales and special events open to the public. Let me introduce you to antiques dealers who are passionate about art history and store owners with a knack for unearthing the latest must-have object. And a map of the Saint-Ouen flea market will help you find your way around its 1700 dealers.

A leather collar box from 1912 ● station clocks ● Borge Mogensen chairs ● dyed linens in grey and celadon green ● wooden letter printing blocks ● maps and posters ● canvas army camp beds ● a dozen blue-green bottles ● portrait of a lady ● a box of old photos from the seaside ● papier mâché animals

Forme à chaussure
en tilleul
20 €/pr

# Galerie Et Caetera

This exquisite store can be found on Rue du Poitou in the Marais. Owner Franck Delmarcelle is from Belgium, his particular style honed over the years. He is a much admired decorator and antiques dealer, followed for his individual flair and the unique objects he collects.

40 RUE DE POITOU . 75003 . 06 66 92 75 77 . FRANCKDELMARCELLE.COM
MÉTRO SAINT-SÉBASTIEN–FROISSART

3rd
Map p. 264

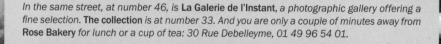

In the same street, at number 46, is **La Galerie de l'Instant**, *a photographic gallery offering a fine selection.* **The collection** *is at number 33. And you are only a couple of minutes away from* **Rose Bakery** *for lunch or a cup of tea: 30 Rue Debelleyme, 01 49 96 54 01.*

# Zut!

In his small store and workshop on Rue Ravignan, just a few metres from **BATEAU LAVOIR**, Frédéric Daniel sells industrial furniture and clocks of all sizes, especially station clocks. You're likely to find him in overalls, busy working, his hands deep in a timepiece. Everything here is on a large scale, each clock is in working order and has its original motor. It's a dream location for fashion photographers.

9 RUE RAVIGNAN . 75018 . 01 42 59 69 68 . ANTIQUITES-INDUSTRIELLES.COM
MÉTRO ABBESSES

*18th*
*Map p.278*

# No Factory

Industrial furniture, tables, chairs and stools come together in this space near the Canal Saint-Martin. Nikolaj has had the store since 2008. *No Factory* is based on the idea of the one-off. While you may find, for example, a batch of identical chairs, the trend is against mass production. Nikolaj finds and restores second-hand pieces and also produces pieces to order, recreating tables based on what he finds but in dimensions tailored to everyday life. His main clients are hotels, restaurants and cafés, and film set decorators come to hire particular pieces.

2 RUE DE L'HÔPITAL SAINT-LOUIS . 75010 . 06 09 64 75 99 . NOFACTORY.FR
MÉTRO COLONEL FABIEN

**10**<sup>th</sup>
*Map p. 274*

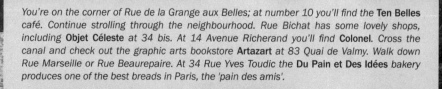

*You're on the corner of Rue de la Grange aux Belles; at number 10 you'll find the **Ten Belles** café. Continue strolling through the neighbourhood. Rue Bichat has some lovely shops, including **Objet Céleste** at 34 bis. At 14 Avenue Richerand you'll find **Colonel**. Cross the canal and check out the graphic arts bookstore **Artazart** at 83 Quai de Valmy. Walk down Rue Marseille or Rue Beaurepaire. At 34 Rue Yves Toudic the **Du Pain et Des Idées** bakery produces one of the best breads in Paris, the 'pain des amis'.*

# Tombées du Camion

Tucked away in Rue Joseph de Maistre, not far from Montmartre and a few steps from the bustling Rue des Abbesses, this little store—*Tombées du Camion*, literally 'fallen off a truck'—definitely warrants a visit. It's the brainchild of Charles Maas, who sells old but unused items dating from 1900 to 1980. Wooden school rulers, toy cars, dolls' eyes, plastic guns, necklaces—trinkets that often tap directly into our memories. The prices are reasonable and the fact that these items come from 'lots' dispels any notion of rarity. Charles also creates graphic wall installations out of his items: the object and its main function disappear as shape and repetition create a new arrangement. You can see the installations at the back of his store, or on the ceiling of the **KILIWATCH** store. They have definitely become Charles' signature pieces.

17 RUE JOSEPH DE MAISTRE . 75018 . 09 81 21 62 80 . TOMBEESDUCAMION.COM
MÉTRO ABBESSES

18*th*
*Map p.278*

# Kidimo

Nicolas Flachot is known for his coloured letters and wordplays that now grace many Parisian apartments. The workshop on Rue Saint-Denis, in the Sentier neighbourhood near Boulevard Sébastopol, is a dream location. It's a space full of light, with a wall of glass windows inside a quiet courtyard where he is free to indulge every new idea. Nicolas gives new life to letters from old business signs and logos that are otherwise destined for the scrapheap. In the workshop, the letters are stacked by size, type and style. You can buy *Kidimo* online, from fashion and design mecca **MERCI** or from the workshop by appointment.

227 RUE SAINT-DENIS . 75002 . KIDIMO.COM
MÉTRO RÉAUMUR–SÉBASTOPOL

**2nd**
*Map p. 262*

*This neighbourhood has many hidden walkways. If you're curious, look for the pretty Passage de l'Ancre, accessible from 223 Rue Saint-Martin or 30 Rue de Turbigo. One of the stores hidden away in this laneway, **Pep's**, sells and repairs umbrellas, parasols and walking sticks. 01 42 78 11 67 . Métro Réaumur–Sébastopol . PEPS-PARIS.COM*

# Jérôme Lepert

Jérôme Lepert is known for his collection of industrial furniture. There are tables, cabinets and especially light fittings—his hanging lamps have become his calling card. Jérôme has also re-released the *Nicolle* stool and chair, which was designed to meet new safety and comfort standards set in the early twentieth century.

106 RUE VIEILLE DU TEMPLE . 75003 . 06 10 18 18 88
MÉTRO SAINT-SÉBASTIEN–FROISSART

3rd
Map p.264

# L'Oeil du Pélican

On the corner of Rue du Pélican in Paris' 1st arrondissement is a quiet and relaxing little shop. There's stuff everywhere; it's a bit like a flea market where you need to rummage before suddenly stumbling on something amazing. There are fragile and unusual items, such as an old herbarium or a packet of sugared almonds from 1927 accompanied by a handwritten letter. Lozenge tins, sewing paraphernalia and a lovely spice cabinet rub shoulders on the shop's two floors.

In a similar vein, at 1 Rue d'Alençon in the 15th arrondissement is **FANETTE**, a store that offers an elegant selection of antiques. You'll find white-glass milk bottles, blue kelsch linen from Alsace and fine old baskets. It's a sure thing you'll find something amazing here.

13 RUE JEAN-JACQUES ROUSSEAU . 75001 . 01 40 13 70 00 . LOEILDUPELICAN.FR
MÉTRO LOUVRE-RIVOLI

1st
Map p. 260

On the same street, at number 14, is **Claus**, a café and grocery store that specialises in breakfast foods. CLAUSPARIS.COM And don't miss Galérie Vero Dodat, a beautiful covered walkway filled with designer boutiques, including **Christian Louboutin**.

# Anna Colore

Anna is Italian. Based in Rue Paul Bert in the 11th arrondissement, she sells a variety of metal objects, letters, chairs, children's furniture and toys, stools and light fittings, such as clamp spotlights. This is also the place to come for beautiful *Lalampawill* lamps.

7 RUE PAUL BERT . 75011 . 01 43 79 41 62 . ANNA-COLORE-INDUSTRIALE.COM

MÉTRO FAIDHERBE-CHALIGNY

**11th**
*Map p.276*

# Au Petit Bonheur la Chance

School notebooks, pencil boxes, old flour bags, chocolate moulds, earthenware café au lait bowls. Piles of old tea towels with blue stripes, red stripes and floral patterns. Old school geography maps, embroidered towels and old toys. *Au Petit Bonheur la Chance* brings together childhood objects of yesteryear. It's a tiny shop with a wide range and lots of memories.

13 RUE SAINT-PAUL . 75004 . 01 42 74 36 38
MÉTRO PONT MARIE

4<sup>th</sup>
Map p. 266

# Broc Martel

Laurence Peyrelade is a fan of the 10th arrondissement. The store where she set up her business had been used as a storeroom for an electrician and the metal roller door had not been opened since 1941! Dusted off and freshened up, the shop now sells furniture dating from 1930 to 1960. Laurence clearly has a soft spot for fairground pieces and chairs. The fairground items are quite amazing: merry-go-round horses, a phenomenal rooster, a 2.5-metre carousel swallow and a 4.5-metre painted canvas advertising a Siamese twins exhibit in the United States in the early 1800s. Chairs are Laurence's second passion: they are all originals, with names such as *Flambo*, *Nicolle*, *Tolix* and *Biénaise*. She's had to start up a second store—called, predictably, *Chairs*—at the other end of the street, but it's open only by appointment.

12 RUE MARTEL . 75010 . 01 48 24 53 43 . BROCMARTEL.COM
MÉTRO CHÂTEAU D'EAU

**10th** Map p. 274

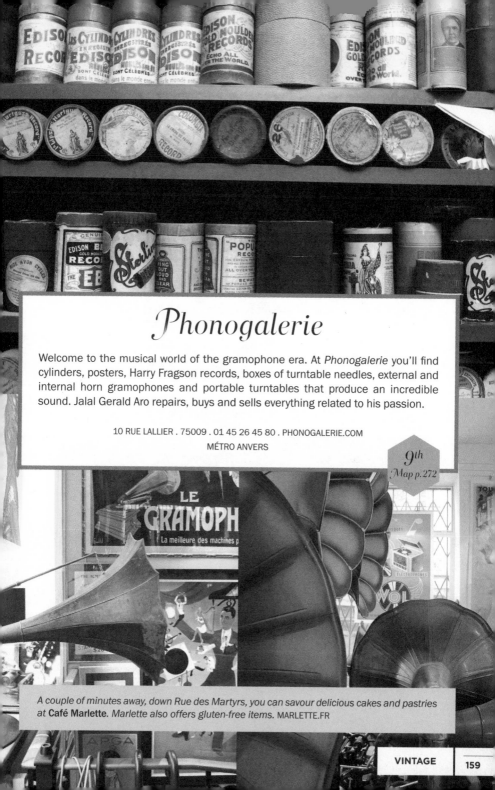

# Phonogalerie

Welcome to the musical world of the gramophone era. At *Phonogalerie* you'll find cylinders, posters, Harry Fragson records, boxes of turntable needles, external and internal horn gramophones and portable turntables that produce an incredible sound. Jalal Gerald Aro repairs, buys and sells everything related to his passion.

10 RUE LALLIER . 75009 . 01 45 26 45 80 . PHONOGALERIE.COM
MÉTRO ANVERS

9th
*Map p.272*

*A couple of minutes away, down Rue des Martyrs, you can savour delicious cakes and pastries at Café Marlette. Marlette also offers gluten-free items.* MARLETTE.FR

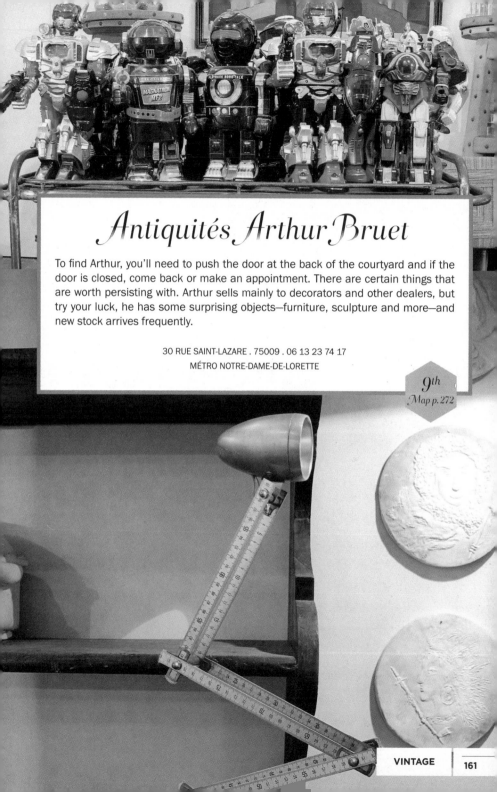

# Antiquités Arthur Bruet

To find Arthur, you'll need to push the door at the back of the courtyard and if the door is closed, come back or make an appointment. There are certain things that are worth persisting with. Arthur sells mainly to decorators and other dealers, but try your luck, he has some surprising objects—furniture, sculpture and more—and new stock arrives frequently.

30 RUE SAINT-LAZARE . 75009 . 06 13 23 74 17
MÉTRO NOTRE-DAME-DE-LORETTE

*9th*
*Map p. 272*

# Marion Held Javal

A few paces from the Odéon theatre, Marion Held Javal has arranged over two floors a collection of objects, each more surprising than the last. You'll find papier mâché animals, a stuffed bear and some beautiful pieces of tableware in the back room. The store also sells superb furniture by architect and designer Marc Held.

21 RUE DE L'ODÉON . 75006 . 01 43 29 96 91
MÉTRO ODÉON

6<sup>th</sup>
Map p. 268

Down the street, heading towards Boulevard Saint-Germain, you'll find **Le Comptoir** restaurant. They don't take reservations, so join the queue. Bide your time with a pre-dinner drink at **L'Avant Comptoir**, which is right next door.

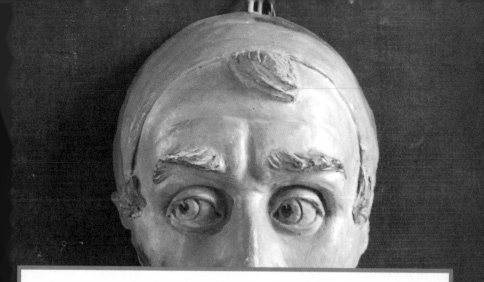

# Yveline

On the pretty Rue Furstemberg in the Saint-Germain-des-Prés neighbourhood you'll find the **MUSÉE EUGÈNE DELACROIX**, the magnificent **FLAMANT** boutique, **MAISON DU CHOU** pâtisserie, **OSBORNE & LITTLE** wallpapers and, since 1954, *Yveline*'s cabinet of curiosities. I love coming here; there are full-size articulated wooden mannequins once used by painters, old aviator sunglasses ... it's a mixture of objects, paintings and furniture that's unique and difficult to find elsewhere.

4 RUE DE FURSTEMBERG . 75006 . 01 43 26 56 91 . YVELINE-ANTIQUITES.COM
MÉTRO SAINT-GERMAIN-DES-PRÉS

6<sup>th</sup>
Map p. 268

# Dank

Post-war Scandinavian furniture; original pieces by Hans Wegner, Grete Jalk or Ilmari Tiapovaraa, all in perfect condition; light fittings and a lovely collection of ceramics. François-Xavier Dousset refreshes his selection once or twice a month. The store is close to the stately Avenue Trudaine.

8 RUE BOCHART DE SARON . 75009 . 06 74 58 11 91 . DANK.FR
MÉTRO ANVERS

$9^{th}$
Map p. 272

Take a look at the superb design revue **The Drawer** at number 6, and if you find yourself in the area towards the end of the day, **Artisan** bar at number 14 makes fabulous cocktails.

# La Galerie Salon

This small boutique, tucked away in the Saint-Germain-des-Prés neighbourhood, offers a broad selection of **ASTIER DE VILLATTE** tableware and superb antiques.

4 RUE DE BOURBON-LE-CHÂTEAU . 75006 . 06 33 85 98 99
MÉTRO SAINT-GERMAIN-DES-PRÉS

6th
Map p. 268

# La Galcante

I came across this place completely by chance. It's a bookshop hidden inside a courtyard, a space dedicated to old French and international print media. Each shelf is filled with newspapers, papers and posters, perfectly categorised by topic and year—the old-school way, not computerised. You'll find back issues of *Vogue* with illustrated covers; and issues of *L'Œil*, an art journal founded in 1955 with contributions from leading art-world figures, such as designer Andrée Putman and photographer Robert Doisneau. It's a gold mine.

52 RUE DE L'ARBRE SEC . 75001 . 01 44 77 87 44 . LAGALCANTE.COM
MÉTRO TUILERIES

1*st*
Map p. 260

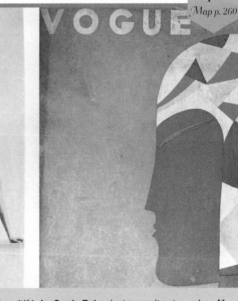

In the evening, the ideal place for an aperitif is **Le Garde Robe**, *just opposite at number 41.*

# Librairie Alain Brieux

A fascinating bookshop specialising in science and medicine. It has manuals on occult sciences, such as alchemy, but also technical manuals on computing machines and steam engines, guides to botany and crystallography, posters and a whole assortment of surprising objects, including anatomical models. Displayed in the window are Cardan's famous *Métoposcopie* and anatomical charts.

48 RUE JACOB . 75006 . 01 42 60 21 98 . ALAINBRIEUX.COM

MÉTRO MABILLON

*6th*
*Map p. 268*

Fig. 3.

Fig. 5.

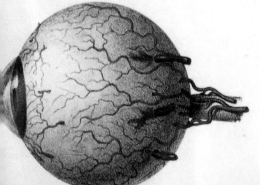

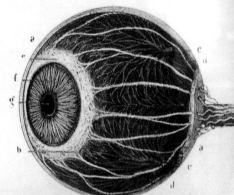

# Librairie Elbé

The *Elbé* bookstore specialises in travel posters and prints. Poster art developed in France from 1880, then took off with the beginning of colonisation and the craze for travel and the exotic. In 1930, it took eleven days to reach Saigon from Paris by plane, with many stops along the way, and twelve days to travel from London to Aswan on the Orient Express. Posters were used to inspire travel to exotic places, but also to promote France abroad. Toulouse-Lautrec, Villemot, Eugène Ogé and Savignac are just some of the famous names who employed their skills for poster art. The bookstore sells linen-backed posters, buys posters and researches specific topics on request. It ships internationally.

213 BOULEVARD SAINT-GERMAIN . 75007 . 01 45 48 77 97 . ELBE-PARIS.FR
MÉTRO RUE DU BAC

*7th*
*Map p. 270*

# Puces de Saint-Ouen

This flea market began to take shape in the late nineteenth century. The Malassis area, which for a long time had been a tax-free zone mainly occupied by gypsy caravans, started to attract more and more people. Ragpickers and other junk dealers who salvaged discarded objects gradually moved here, away from the centre of Paris, after decrees made it obligatory for every Parisian household to have a garbage container, thus depriving them of their livelihood. The area became lively with gypsy music and bistros, a place where objects and clothes—fleas included—were bought and sold. Stalls went up, the ragpickers became second-hand dealers and successive newcomers have taken the place of the old guard. The flea market has evolved, but it still offers incredible stories, characters and an element of random luck.

# Puces de Saint-Ouen

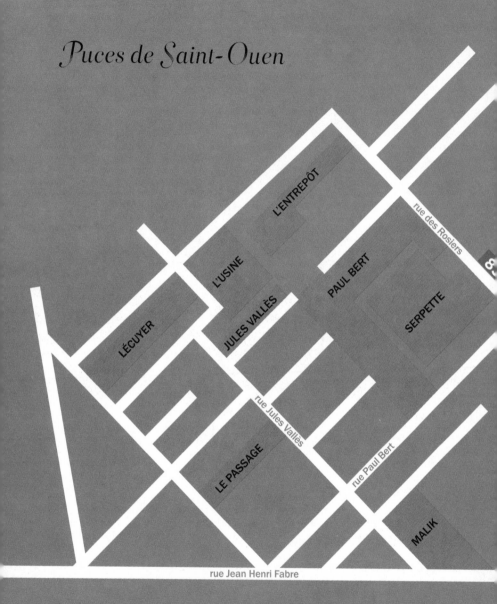

L'ENTREPÔT

rue des Rosiers

85

L'USINE

PAUL BERT

JULES VALLÈS

SERPETTE

LÉCUYER

rue Jules Vallès

LE PASSAGE

rue Paul Bert

MALIK

rue Jean Henri Fabre

 MÉTRO PORTE DE CLIGNANCOURT

**85** BUS LINE 85 MAIRIE DE SAINT-OUEN–LUXEMBOURG

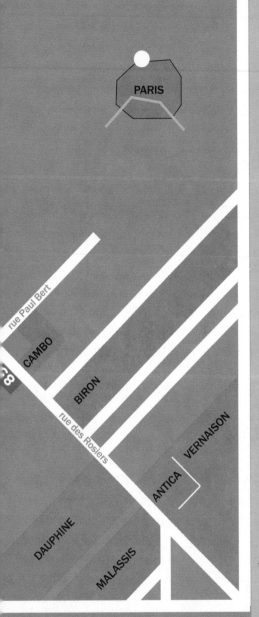

**ANTICA:** eighteenth- and nineteenth-century furniture and objects.

**BIRON:** furniture from Europe and Asia; jewellery, graphic arts from eighteenth-century to twentieth-century design.

**CAMBO:** eighteenth- and nineteenth-century furniture, paintings and objects; old weapons, curio cabinets, Scandinavian furniture.

**DAUPHINE:** classic antiques, furniture and vintage fashion; industrial design, booksellers, stalls specialising in music, textiles, watches and jewellery, crafts.

**L'ENTREPÔT:** large-scale objects, such as staircases, fireplaces, libraries ...

**JULES VALLÈS:** old furniture and objects, Art Nouveau and twentieth-century design, bronze, clocks and watches, vintage books, posters, records, militaria.

**LÉCUYER** and **L'USINE:** for professional dealers only.

**MALASSIS:** pieces from antiquity to contemporary times; Asian and Middle Eastern art, Art Deco, twentieth-century design, bronze, erotica, books, toys, fashion, photos, sculptures, European glassware.

**MALIK:** new clothes, fashion designers.

**LE PASSAGE:** books, postcards, stylish garden furniture, old clothes.

**PAUL BERT:** furniture, art and decorative objects from seventeenth-century to vintage.

**SERPETTE:** high-end objects, antiquity to the 1970s.

**VERNAISON:** antique and vintage objects, tableware, furniture from the eighteenth to the twentieth century, unusual objects.

**OPENING HOURS**
SATURDAYS 10 AM–5.30 PM
SUNDAYS 10 AM–5.30 PM
MONDAYS 11 AM–5 PM

Puces de
St-Ouen

# Ludovic Messager

There's electronic music playing over two levels and an amazing assembly of
objects, each more surprising than the last.

QUINTESSENCE PLAYGROUND . MARCHÉ PAUL BERT . 3 RUE PAUL BERT . 06 18 99 18 25

# Dugay

Mainly a supplier of products to maintain and restore old furniture and art objects. You can also find fabric-covered electrical cords and decorative light bulbs.

92 RUE DES ROSIERS . 01 40 11 87 30 . PRODUITS-DUGAY.COM

# Un Singe en Hiver

Garden furniture and decorative objects in a beautiful house built in 1909.

MARCHÉ PAUL BERT . 6 RUE PAUL BERT . 06 75 55 44 57 . UNSINGENHIVER.COM

# La Petite Maison

Not to be missed—beautiful furniture and superb figure drawings in a lovely house.

MARCHÉ PAUL BERT . 10 RUE PAUL BERT . 01 40 10 56 69

Puces de St-Ouen

# Colonial Concept

The incredible displays at the *Colonial Concept* store are something to see.

MARCHÉ PAUL BERT . 8 RUE PAUL BERT . 01 40 10 00 71 . FRANCOISDANECK.COM

# Untitled

*Untitled* sells old clothes and fabrics and true denim (*de Nîmes*). It's a collection centred around workwear and exploring the soul of the piece of clothing through the person who wore it.

MARCHÉ PAUL BERT . 96 RUE DES ROSIERS . ALLÉE 1, STAND 122
UNTITLED-CLOTHES.FR

## *The Duke*

*The* specialist in American vintage that lures Ralph Lauren across the Atlantic as well as many other fashion figures.

MARCHÉ VERNAISON . 99 RUE DES ROSIERS . ALLÉE 1, STAND 37 . 06 32 37 17 11

## *Elodie Sanson*

A beautiful selection of tribal art objects, jewellery and photographs.

MARCHÉ VERNAISON . ALLÉE 2, STAND 51 BIS . 06 10 01 38 97

Puces de
St-Ouen

# Bachelier

Specialises in food and wine-related antiques: copper pots, bottles, terrines ...

MARCHÉ PAUL BERT . 18 RUE PAUL BERT . ALLÉE 1, STAND 17
01 40 11 89 98 . BACHELIER-ANTIQUITES.COM

# Mathias Roudine

Mathias Roudine offers an original collection—old panoramic photos, a set of letters more than 1.5 metres tall, and railway and navigation-related objects.

MARCHÉ PAUL BERT . 96 RUE DES ROSIERS . ALLÉE 5, STAND 247 . 06 20 63 06 94

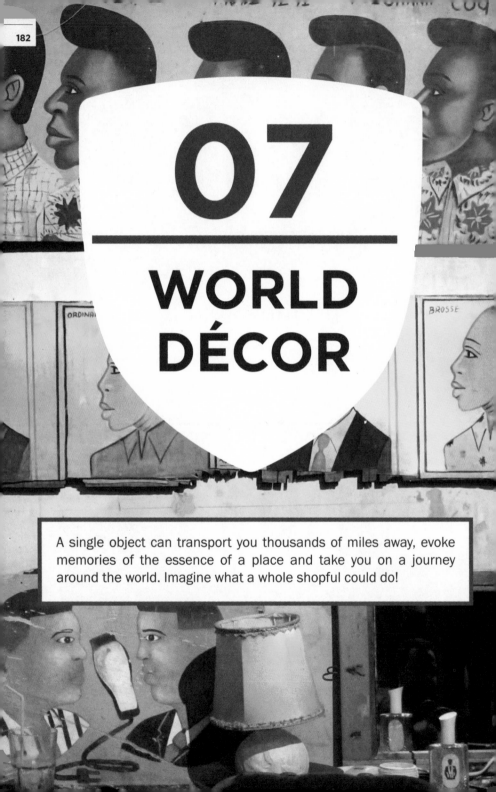

# 07

## WORLD DÉCOR

A single object can transport you thousands of miles away, evoke memories of the essence of a place and take you on a journey around the world. Imagine what a whole shopful could do!

Woven baskets • Indigo cushions to doze on • smells of incense • enamelled dishes with green accents for serving a pad thai • a coloured metal suitcase for organising your bracelets • photos and souvenirs • citrus scents recreating a Moroccan riad

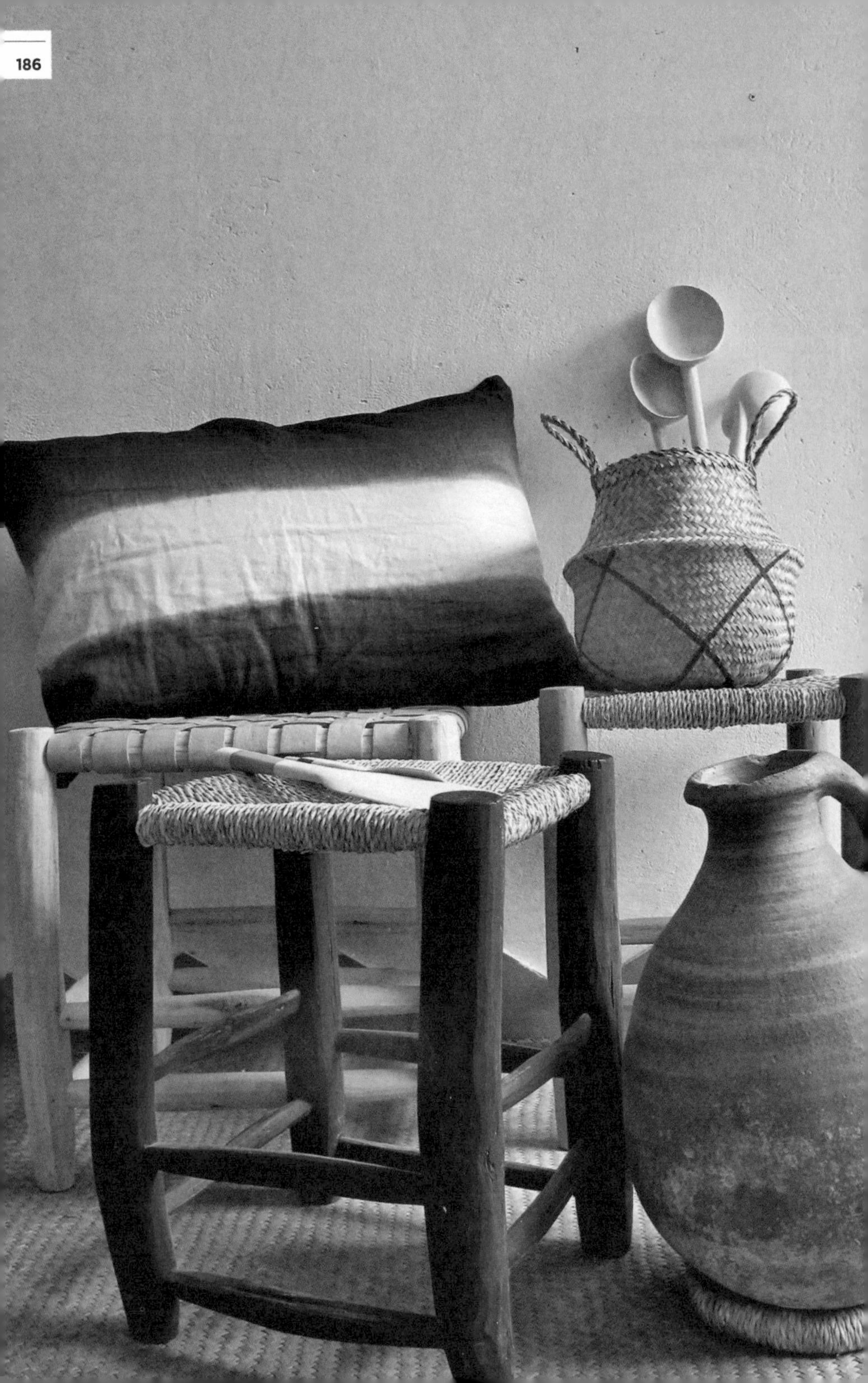

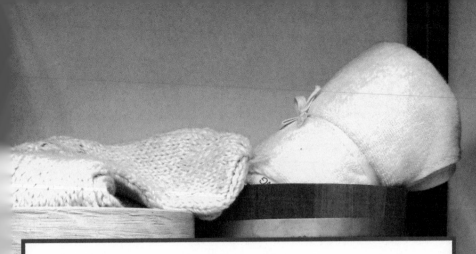

# Baan

The *Baan* brand was created by Clémentine, a great traveller and tireless treasure hunter. She brings back old and new objects and accessories from her various travels in South-East Asia and Morocco, where she works in collaboration with local artisans. Utilising traditional techniques, she has developed a line of baskets and painted stools.

At *Baan*, you'll find a broad range of basketwork, jewellery (like the Padaung bracelets), traditional Thai brass woks and lots of kitchenware. Some prestigious establishments, such as the *Conran Shop*, buy stock from here. The showroom is on the periphery of Paris and can be visited by appointment. *Baan* has an online shop and delivers both within France and overseas.

13 RUE LA RÉVOLUTION . 94200 . IVRY-SUR-SEINE . 06 23 46 09 61
BAAN-BAAN.COM . RER IVRY-SUR-SEINE

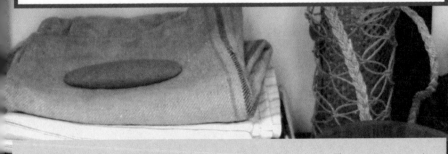

*Usha Bora's lovely store, **Jamini**, in Rue du Château d'Eau in the 10th arrondissement, is certainly worth a visit. It has collections of cushions, notebooks, scarves and bags that Usha commissions from India, where she was born. She works with artisans in different regions who've been able to preserve ancestral techniques of weaving and printing cottons, wools and silks. The fabrics are wonderfully soft and the prices very affordable.*

# Le Comptoir Général

What an amazing place! It has a small cinema, exhibitions, concerts, a second-hand clothes store, a snack bar... *Le Comptoir Général* is a meeting place in constant flux. It champions exotic, marginalised and disadvantaged cultures. The space is enormous. From Monday to Thursday, *Le Comptoir* is used by groups concerned with issues of the environment, solidarity, social innovation and global perspectives. It's open to the public from Thursday evening and all weekend. Come for brunch or one of the many evening events. But go easy on the Secousse cocktail, a house speciality made from hibiscus juice, cucumber, vodka and passionfruit.

80 QUAI DE JEMMAPES . 75010 . 01 44 88 20 45
LECOMPTOIRGENERAL.COM . MÉTRO JACQUES BONSERGENT

*10th*
*Map p. 274*

# CSAO

This is the place for pretty plastic woven mats. They come in different sizes, various patterns and many colours. The *Compagnie du Sénégal et de l'Afrique de l'Ouest* set itself up in the Marais in 1997 and sells decorative objects and furniture from West Africa. Valérie Schlumberger, who lived for a long time in Senegal, has forged ties with African artisans and sells their work in her two shops. The selection includes cushions, bedspreads and beautiful *Jokko* necklaces and bracelets.

9 RUE ELZÉVIR . 75003 . 01 42 71 33 17 . CSAO.FR
MÉTRO CHEMIN VERT

**3rd**
*Map p. 264*

*Rue Elzévir also offers an African restaurant, **Le Petit Dakar**, and a bar, **Jokko**, created in association with Senegalese singer Youssou N'Dour.*

# The Appointment

*The Appointment* sells Philippe Xerri's *Rock the Kasbah* label, furniture designed by Philippe Xerri and produced by Tunisian artisans. There are kilim-covered cushions, armchairs, sofas and ceramics. Philippe Xerri was recently involved in the decoration of **LE PERCHOIR**'s roof-top bar, the ideal place for long summer evenings.

14 RUE BEAUREGARD . 75002 . MÉTRO BONNE NOUVELLE

*12th*

# C&P

I visit *C&P* in Rue du Pont Louis-Philippe for their beautiful wooden boards, scissors and small Moroccan handicrafts and to check on what's recently arrived. Everyday objects are beautifully crafted and you are guaranteed to find something lovely.

16 RUE DU PONT LOUIS-PHILIPPE . 75004 . 01 42 74 22 34
MÉTRO SAINT-PAUL

4<sup>th</sup>

*Map p.266*

*Further along the same street, at number 3, **Fouta Tunisie** is a small shop selling Tunisian foutas—woven cotton towels. Green ones, yellow ones, pink ones ... all beautiful quality.*

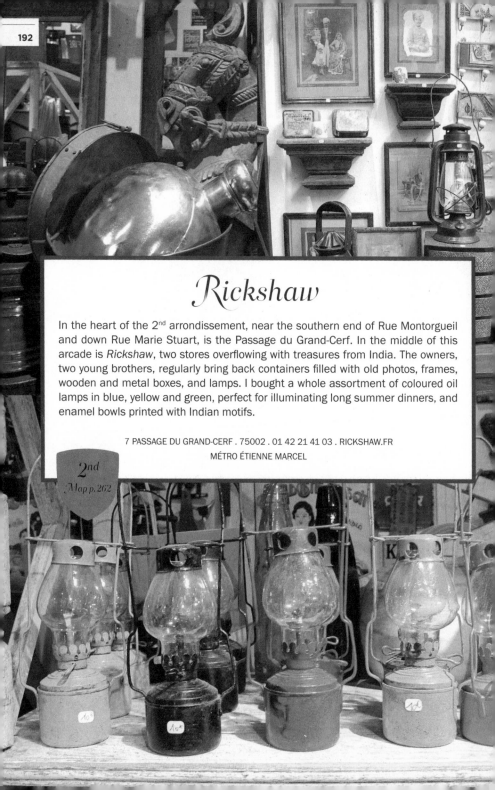

# Rickshaw

In the heart of the 2nd arrondissement, near the southern end of Rue Montorgueil and down Rue Marie Stuart, is the Passage du Grand-Cerf. In the middle of this arcade is *Rickshaw*, two stores overflowing with treasures from India. The owners, two young brothers, regularly bring back containers filled with old photos, frames, wooden and metal boxes, and lamps. I bought a whole assortment of coloured oil lamps in blue, yellow and green, perfect for illuminating long summer dinners, and enamel bowls printed with Indian motifs.

7 PASSAGE DU GRAND-CERF . 75002 . 01 42 21 41 03 . RICKSHAW.FR

MÉTRO ÉTIENNE MARCEL

2nd

*Map p. 262*

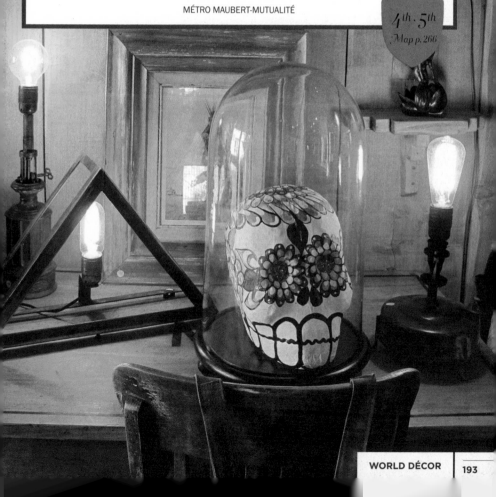

# La Cabane de l'Ours

Hidden in the courtyard of the Village Saint-Paul is *La Cabane de l'Ours*. It's a place dedicated to the spirit of the American log cabin, with *Pendleton San Miguel* rugs and blankets, combining the traditional weaving of nineteenth-century Native Americans and the influence of Spanish missionaries; hand-painted Mexican papier mâché masks; mirrors, frames and furniture. In the 5th arrondissement, **GALERIE URUBAMBA** specialises in the cultures of North, Central and South American Indians. It has photos, objects and books on the subject.

VILLAGE SAINT-PAUL . 23 RUE SAINT-PAUL . 75004 . 01 42 71 01 49
LACABANEDELOURS.COM . MÉTRO SAINT-PAUL
GALERIE URUBAMBA: 4 RUE DE LA BÛCHERIE . 75005 . 01 43 54 08 24
MÉTRO MAUBERT-MUTUALITÉ

4th · 5th
Map p. 266

# C𝓕OC

*La Compagnie Française de l'Orient et de la Chine* has had a makeover with the help of **SARAH LAVOINE** and now offers a total lifestyle in its sublime Boulevard Haussmann boutique: a restaurant, exhibitions, high-quality tableware, linens, stationery and contemporary and original furniture. You can find designer pieces, such as *Celine Wright* lamps and *Benjamin* furniture. *CFOC* draws on traditional craftsmanship and increasingly prefers to work on small series of objects, lines produced specifically for *CFOC*.

260 BOULEVARD SAINT-GERMAIN . 75007 . 01 47 05 92 82 . MÉTRO SOLFÉRINO
170 BOULEVARD HAUSSMANN . 75008 . 01 53 53 40 80
CFOC.FR . MÉTRO MIROMESNIL

7ᵗʰ . 8ᵗʰ
*Map p. 270*

*The store on Boulevard Haussmann is just 800 metres from the **Espace Culturel Louis Vuitton**, which offers regular travel-related exhibitions. The venue is open from noon till 7 pm. 60 Rue de Bassano . 01 53 57 52 03 . LOUISVUITTON-ESPACECULTUREL.COM*

# Mahatsara

This is a basket mecca. Here you will find South African baskets made from crocheted hemp, *Binky Newman* basketware in different plant fibres and colourful Zulu baskets fashioned from telephone wire. There are also hanging lamps, cushions and white and copper-coloured bowls made from recycled magazines in Swaziland and water-resistant thanks to a non-toxic varnish.

8 RUE OBERKAMPF . 75011 . 01 58 30 89 29 . MAHATSARA.COM
MÉTRO OBERKAMPF

11th
Map p.276

# Ouma Productions

Stéphanie de Saint-Simon worked in events for over 20 years, creating environments for different clients. Today, having travelled extensively in India, she brings back furniture and objects that she sells as they are, or uses as inspiration for new pieces adapted to Parisian interiors. Her coloured metal suitcases and stools and her charpoys—woven Indian street beds—have become part of her design signature. You can find *Ouma Productions* items in various stores in Paris, such as **CARAVANE** and *Autruches*. Or you can make an appointment directly with Stéphanie.

BY APPOINTMENT . 8 IMPASSE SAINT-SÉBASTIEN . 75011
06 14 31 32 48 . OUMAPRODUCTIONS.COM . MÉTRO RICHARD-LENOIR

*11th*
*Map p. 276*

# 08

## TABLE

Most kitchenware stores are concentrated around Les Halles—a neighbourhood that, until 1969, was home to the capital's largest food market, before its relocation to the south of Paris. Shops specialising in tableware, on the other hand, can be found all over Paris. Department stores also offer a wide range, but it's often the smaller shops that have innovative selections and pieces you won't see anywhere else. Here are my favourite places.

Cream horn cones ■ shepherd's knife ■ an Eiffel Tower mould ■ Vichy nonnette rings in stainless steel ■ hardware luxe ■ paring knives ■ vintage bowls ■ a Japanese teapot ■ caramel you can pour ■ silver lustre ■ fluted brioche tins ■ fine tableware ■ sparkling cutlery

TABLE 201

# Merci

It is impossible not to mention *Merci* when talking about shops in Paris. But it's also a challenge to choose just one section of this book to put it in. This Parisian concept store covers every aspect of lifestyle—bedroom, living room, cosmetics, stationery, lighting, fashion and, of course, the kitchen and dining room. *Merci* offers a particularly wide and interesting range. In the basement you'll find kitchenware, much of it from abroad—Scandinavia, Japan—and exclusive to *Merci*. The selection is modern, attractive and above all practical. You'll find the *Malle W. Trousseau* collection here. On the first floor is glassware, crockery and cutlery. The pieces are displayed in perfect arrangements. I go there especially for cutlery from the Portuguese brand *Cutipol*, linen serviettes and blown glassware from *Soufflerie*. Products from *Merci* are now available online.

111 BOULEVARD BEAUMARCHAIS . 75003 . 01 42 77 00 33 . MERCI-MERCI.COM
MÉTRO FILLES DU CALVAIRE

3rd
Map.p.264

*As you leave* **Merci**, *in front of the Saint-Sébastien–Froissart metro station you'll find* **Blend**, *which serves excellent burgers. 1 Boulevard des Filles du Calvaire* . BLENDHAMBURGER.COM

TABLE    203

# E. Dehillerin

Famous among food lovers all over the world for its window display, *E. Dehillerin* is a Parisian institution. The store reflects the old Paris. On the unvarnished wooden shelves are implements that have all but disappeared with the evolution of cooking. Attelets, for example, a sort of metal skewer topped with an ornamental hare, rooster or pig, once used for fancy dishes like *canard à l'orange*. There are no electrical gadgets here, it is a temple to traditional cuisine—copper tarte tatin moulds, charlotte moulds, knives, roasting trays and giant saucepans. The place is usually packed, so be patient. And it closes at 6 pm sharp.

18-20 RUE COQUILLIÈRE . 75001 . 01 42 36 53 13 . E-DEHILLERIN.FR
MÉTRO ÉTIENNE MARCEL OR LES HALLES

1st
Map p. 260

---

*Close by, at 15 Rue du Louvre,* **La Verrerie des Halles** *specialises in all kinds of tableware and jars.* 01 42 36 86 02 . VERRERIE-DES-HALLES-PARIS.FR

TABLE 205

# G. Detou

Don't miss the *G. Detou* food store. With no pun intended, *G. Detou* really has it '*tout*' (all)—all the best-quality products from France and elsewhere, from *pieds paquets* (an offal delicacy from Marseille) to dried morel mushrooms and a 5-kilogram slab of *Valrhona* chocolate. It's a paradise for cooks.

58 RUE TIQUETONNE . 75002 . 01 42 36 54 67 . GDETOU.COM
MÉTRO ÉTIENNE MARCEL OR LES HALLES

2nd
Map p. 262

# Mora

This is another great meeting place for cooks in Paris. At *Mora* you'll find a wide range of products, especially moulds, including a *Tour Eiffel* mould. It has a more modern selection than **E. DEHILLERIN**. There are cupcake decorating accessories, everything related to pastry and baking, tray moulds and kitchen appliances.

13 RUE MONTMARTRE . 75001 . 01 45 08 19 24 . MORA.FR
MÉTRO ÉTIENNE MARCEL OR LES HALLES

1*st*
*Map p. 260*

*Rue Montmartre has a series of specialist kitchenware stores, so have a good wander through the neighbourhood.* **Déco'Relief**, *at number 6, sells all kinds of silicone cake moulds and cake decorations.* **A. Simon** *is at number 48, and at the corner of Rue Etienne Marcel is* **La Bovida**.

TABLE 207

# Ceccaldi

Mr Ceccaldi is Corsican. With other members of his family he creates exceptional knives—folding and non-folding shepherd's knives, kitchen and table knives—in his Porto-Vecchio workshop. The shape of the wood dictates the design of the knife, so each piece has its own identity. The store in Rue Racine, close to the Odéon, also contains a workshop with a knife-sharpening service. You can now also buy knives engraved by young designer Elodie Di Battista.

15 RUE RACINE . 75006 . 01 46 33 87 20 . COUTEAUX-CECCALDI.COM
MÉTRO ODÉON

6th
Map p. 268

TABLE    209

# Corner Shop

This little shop is in the Village Saint-Paul on the corner of the Quai des Célestins. I go there for designer products that only they carry, such as *Pauline Deltour's* Roulé trays, magnificent Italian glasses and special Japanese teapots.

For more designer tableware, visit **XANADOU** in the 6th arrondissement, **UP** in the 3rd and **ZERO ONE ONE** in the 1st.

3 RUE SAINT-PAUL . 75004 . 01 42 77 50 88
MÉTRO PONT MARIE

4th
*Map p. 266*

*If you are passionate about old chairs, at 21 Rue Saint-Paul you'll discover* **Au Bon Usage**, *a shop specialising in Thonet chairs.*

# Perigot

*Perigot* is a French company that has taken the hardware store and breathed new aesthetic life into it. Quality products in attractive designs, from a string dispenser to a vegetable brush or a waterproof market trolley. This is luxury hardware—beautiful and practical.

16 BOULEVARD DES CAPUCINES . 75009 . 01 53 40 98 90 . PERIGOT.FR
MÉTRO OPÉRA

9<sup>th</sup>
Map p. 272

TABLE 211

# Argenterie d'Antan

In Rue de Birague, close to the Marais, Corinne Javaloyès specialises in silver cutlery sets. You'll also find beautiful old pieces that look like new, bearing the names of great French silverware houses. Discontinued *Christofle* collections are ideal for completing a set. The store also offers a polishing service to help restore the lustre of cutlery that has tarnished over time.

6 RUE DE BIRAGUE . 75004 . 01 42 71 31 91 . ARGENTERIE-DANTAN.COM
MÉTRO SAINT-PAUL

4th
Map p. 266

# Tsé ⋄ Tsé

*Tsé & Tsé* sells designer objects, such as their 'famished' plates, 'fingerprint' decanters and 'tipsy' glasses, but also beautiful vintage bowls from Turkey. The store is located right next door to the **SARAH LAVOINE** store.

7 RUE SAINT-ROCH . 75001 . 01 42 61 90 26 . TSE-TSE.COM
MÉTRO TUILERIES

1st
*Map p. 260*

**TABLE** 213

# Caravane Emporium

There's a **CARAVANE** style for every room in the house. In its *Emporium* store in Rue Saint-Nicolas, opposite its *Chambre 19* store, *Caravane* turns its attention to tableware. Black plates and dishes from the *ABC* label, created by the talented Nelson Sepulveda, mingle with objects collected on exotic journeys. You can find rust-coloured ceramic plates from India, an enamel lunch box and blown glassware as well as beautiful *Caravane*-brand tablecloths and napkins. And check out the chic cutlery in hammered or silverplated metal.

22 RUE SAINT-NICOLAS . 75012 . 01 53 17 18 55 . CARAVANE.FR
MÉTRO LEDRU-ROLLIN

*12ᵗʰ*

# À Ma Table

This innovative store near Avenue Trudaine sells tableware, particularly dinner sets that you won't find anywhere else in Paris. It's an attractive selection in simple white or decorated porcelain, with some from abroad, including Italy and Japan.

In Avenue Trudaine, check out **LES COMMIS**. It's the IKEA concept applied to cooking: a Michelin-starred chef puts together a meal that you cook at home. Everything is weighed out, cut up, prepped and ready to go. It's really easy, delicious and fun—something different to do with friends or for a special event.

72 RUE DES MARTYRS . 75009 . A-MA-TABLE.FR . MÉTRO PIGALLE

LES COMMIS: 51 AVENUE TRUDAINE . 75009

01 48 74 83 14 . LESCOMMIS.COM

9th
Map p. 272

TABLE          215

# La Maison de la Porcelaine

Rue du Paradis was once the crystal and porcelain hub of Paris because of its proximity to the Gare de l'Est. The short distance to transport the fragile goods meant fewer breakages. Two stores have survived, *La Maison de la Porcelaine* and **LA CRISTALLERIE DE PARIS**. They offer a huge selection of mainly French pieces. Covering a vast floor space, *La Maison de la Porcelaine* has tableware from Limoges, white pieces of every kind and glassware. *La Cristallerie de Paris* has a more upmarket range, with names such as *Baccarat*, *Bernardaud*, *Christofle*, *Deshoulières* and *Ercuis*.

21 RUE DE PARADIS . 75010 . 01 47 70 22 80

MÉTRO CADET OR CHÂTEAU D'EAU

*10th*

*Map p.274*

*In the same street, the façade of number 18 is covered with decorative tiles. It was once the headquarters and store of the Choisy-le-Roi faïence factory, which notably produced the famous white bevelled tiles of the Paris metro.*

# Fleux

*Fleux* has taken over Rue Sainte-Croix-de-la-Bretonnerie, with four stores facing each other. They offer a vast and varied selection, with stock changing regularly: gadgets and novel decorative accessories, articulated wooden hands, baskets woven from fibre or metal, plateware, furniture, including the *Tolix* label, and stationery. You simply must have a rummage around. In its eccentric collection there's something to suit everyone and at a reasonable price.

39 & 52 RUE SAINTE-CROIX-DE-LA-BRETONNERIE . 75004 . 01 42 78 27 20
FLEUX.COM . MÉTRO HÔTEL DE VILLE

4$^{th}$
*Map p. 266*

TABLE | 217

# Astier de Villatte

The *Astier de Villatte* pieces are made in its workshop on the outskirts of Paris. The shop in Rue Saint-Honoré is gloriously original, the serving dishes, plates and teacups conjuring images of a grand family home. *Astier* evokes a vintage style but with a staunchly modern approach. The materials it utilises—black terracotta with a white glaze—and its collaborations with various decorating figures, such as *John Derian,* place it among the avant-garde. *Astier* offers a timeless heritage, but combines easily with modern elements, making it a safe investment.

173 RUE SAINT-HONORÉ . 75001 . 01 42 60 74 13 . ASTIERDEVILLATTE.COM

MÉTRO PALAIS ROYAL—MUSÉE DU LOUVRE

1st Map p. 260

# La Trésorerie

Located a few steps from Place de la République, *La Trésorerie* is an attractive homewares store. Beneath a large glass roof is a generous space dedicated to kitchenware and tableware. It's an interesting selection, reminiscent of traditional French hardware stores, with a wide range of kitchen knives, saucepans, peelers and chopping boards, but also brushes for various purposes, a range of paints, haberdashery and bathroom furniture and accessories. Objects that are useful, simple and beautiful.

11 RUE DU CHÂTEAU D'EAU . 75010 . 0140 40 20 46 . LATRESORERIE.FR
MÉTRO RÉPUBLIQUE

10*th*
Map p. 274

TABLE      219

# 09

## ACCESSORIES

An accessory sets the tone and brings the whole together. In home décor, it can recreate a moment or symbolise a way of life. A bag woven from natural fibres summons faraway islands and a certain freedom. Vintage sunglasses whisper the elegance of a summer in Capri. A ukulele invites you to put your feet up and chill out. Find a funky necklace to hang on the wall beside a frame or create a row of straw hats. Enter these Aladdin's caves to discover recent and vintage treasures to help express your personality and originality.

Golden brass bicycle bell ● braided leather ribbons ● a Yankees badge from 1953 ● a white and gold necklace ● buttons and bows ● vintage sunglasses ● canvas bags ● a silk scarf ● gold and silver thread ● memories

# Ultramod

These are two unmissable stores in Paris for lovers of ribbons, threads, buttons and general haberdashery. The two shops are opposite each other in Rue Monsigny and their décor has not changed since they opened in 1890. You'll find magnificent old ribbons, fabrics, buttons and reels of thread in incredible colours. Everything is organised in old numbered wooden boxes, stacked from floor to ceiling. You'll want to buy it all.

3 & 4 RUE DE CHOISEUL . 75002 . 01 42 96 98 30
MÉTRO BOURSE

2nd
Map p. 262

# La Droguerie de Paris

Located in the Les Halles neighbourhood next to the Église Saint-Eustache, this haberdashery makes the most of its previous incarnation as a butcher's shop. You squeeze up against the old wooden counters to see the fasteners, chains, clasps and cords used for making jewellery. There are myriad beads and a wide selection of ribbons, cotton threads, skeins of wool and alpaca. Be warned: there can sometimes be a long wait as the store attracts lots of people.

9 & 11 RUE DU JOUR . 75001 . 01 45 08 93 27 . LADROGUERIE.COM
MÉTRO LES HALLES

1st
Map p.260

*If it's open, take a look inside the Église Saint-Eustache. Located in the heart of the Les Halles neighbourhood, the origins of this church date to the early thirteenth century.*

# Journal Standard de Luxe

This Japanese brand has set up its Paris store in the beautiful Galerie de Montpensier, which runs along the gardens of the Palais Royal. Mina, who manages the store, has an incredible gift for displays. The quality of materials is what first attracted my attention, whether in jeans, bags, hats or scarves. The selection is thoughtful and innovative. Ask to browse through the catalogues: they are beautiful and full of inspiration.

11-12 GALERIE DE MONTPENSIER . 75001 . 01 40 20 90 83
JOURNAL-STANDARD.JP . MÉTRO PALAIS ROYAL–MUSÉE DU LOUVRE

1st
Map p. 260

J.S. L.
JOURNAL STANDARD LUXE
J.S. LUXE

# Pour Vos Beaux Yeux

This little store specialises in vintage spectacles. Tucked away in the Passage du Grand-Cerf, it oozes with style from another era. The tiles, furniture and countertops are the perfect backdrop for the retro-style glasses that could have been worn by Grace Kelly or Audrey Hepburn. You'll find old and original models from the 1920s to the 1980s.

10 PASSAGE DU GRAND-CERF . 75002 . 01 42 36 06 79
POURVOSBEAUXYEUX.COM . MÉTRO SENTIER OR ÉTIENNE MARCEL

**2nd**
*Map p. 262*

# En Selle Marcel

Still in the 2nd arrondissement, and not far from the Passage du Grand-Cerf, is this Parisian store specialising in all things cycling. *En Selle Marcel* has a passion for urban cycling and sells fashion accessories that go with life on two wheels. It has a stylish, masculine vibe, with beautiful canvas bags, attractive bells and leather bike seats. There are also charming cardboard and metal containers from the French brand *Rustines*. You can have your own trusty bicycle repaired on site.

40 RUE TIQUETONNE . 75002 . 01 44 54 06 46

ENSELLEMARCEL.COM . MÉTRO SENTIER OR ÉTIENNE MARCEL

2nd
*Map p. 262*

*If you're looking for vintage clothes, try* **Kiliwatch** *on Rue Tiquetonne. Or the* **Ralph Lauren** *store on Boulevard Saint-Germain—the top floor is devoted to the* **Ralph Lauren Vintage** *collection.*

# Yves Andrieux & Vincent Jalbert

Yves Andrieux and Vincent Jalbert rework old fabrics, mainly army canvas rucksacks, bags, parachutes and tents. Dyes are skilfully added or removed, the colours emerging in shades of grey, khaki, black and ecru. These raw materials are then given new life in their shop and workshop on Rue Charlot, in the Marais, as handbags, jackets and cushions. They have many regulars among their clientele, including Japanese clients who adore the quality of the materials.

55 RUE CHARLOT . 75003 . 01 42 71 19 54 . VINCENTJALBERT.COM
MÉTRO FILLES DU CALVAIRE

3rd
Map p. 264

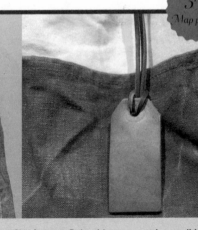

*At number 77 on Rue Charlot, you can buy film for your Polaroid camera at **Impossible**, the Paris incarnation of **The Impossible Project**. This company has revived the production of instant film for these classic cameras.*

# Mokuba

*Mokuba* is a discreet Japanese label ever-present in the defining moments of Paris fashion. At runway shows and on press days you can often spot the little craft paper bag with its black cotton ribbon. *Mokuba* mainly works with haute couture and fashion designers and has more than 50,000 individual items in its catalogue: satins, velvets, taffetas, faux furs, waxed cottons, leathers, lamé, rickrack, braids, pompoms, fringes, sequins, cameos, flowers, frog fastenings and elastics in multiple widths. Don't forget to ask to visit the only showroom in the world dedicated to lace; it's located in a separate space at the back of the store and has 6000 reels of lace in cotton, organdie, silk and netting. If you're inspired, the **LESAGE** embroidery school, in the 9th arrondissement, offers classes for all levels. It has supplied *Chanel* for many years with ribbons and small embroidered accessories.

18 RUE MONTMARTRE . 75001 . 01 40 13 81 41 . MOKUBA.FR
MÉTRO LES HALLES OR ÉTIENNE MARCEL
ÉCOLE LESAGE: 13 RUE DE LA GRANGE BATELIÈRE . 75009
01 44 79 00 88 . LESAGE-PARIS.COM . MÉTRO LE PELETIER

1st
Map p. 260

# Shindo

This is another Japanese haberdashery. However, *Shindo* offers a different range to **MOKUBA**. I come here to look for woollen ribbons and edgings of all kinds and in all colours. Once again, material and colour take centre stage.

2 RUE D'ABOUKIR . 75002 . 01 44 88 27 57 . SHINDO.FR
MÉTRO ÉTIENNE MARCEL

**2nd**
*Map p. 262*

# Khadi and Co

Bess Nielsen is Danish and, led by a spirit of adventure, seems to have roamed the whole world. A love for India led to her fascination with the culture of hand-woven fabrics, in particular *khadi*. Made in India, this cloth was championed by Gandhi—to the point that it became a revolutionary object in defiance of the British system. Its beauty is revealed by Bess through her *Épices* and *Khadi and Co* labels. It comes in cotton, silk or wool, and every season Bess offers new colours.

37 RUE DEBELLEYME . 75003 . 01 42 74 71 32 . KHADIANDCO.COM
MÉTRO FILLES DU CALVAIRE

3<sup>rd</sup>
*Map p. 264*

# Isaac Reina

The pieces at *Isaac Reina* are simple, everyday objects—A4 document holders with elastic closures, toiletry bags, spectacles cases. They are made from beautiful leather, hand crafted and high quality. Isaac Reina worked for eight years as an assistant to Véronique Nichanian, the creative director of the menswear collections at *Hermès*, and launched his first collection in 2006.

38 RUE DE SÉVIGNÉ . 75003 . 01 42 78 81 95 . ISAACREINA.COM
MÉTRO SAINT-PAUL

*Close by at number 44 is* **Le Comptoir de l'Image.** *This bookshop, run by Michael Fink, specialises in photography and attracts collectors, famous photographers and stylists. The shop is filled with books and you may find volumes that are out of print. 01 42 72 03 92*

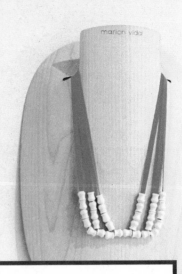

# Marion Vidal

*Marion Vidal's* jewellery is geometric and architectural. It is undoubtedly inspired by the different courses of study she has undertaken. A graduate of fashion from the Antwerp Académie Royale des Beaux-Arts, Marion then turned towards architecture. Her skill in manipulating spaces is paired with a taste for colour and beautiful materials. You'll find matinée necklaces or chokers, which can be worn with simple or formal outfits, bracelets, as well as pieces she has designed for fine French brands, such as *Baccarat*, *Le Bon Marché* and *Christofle*.

13 AVENUE TRUDAINE . 75009 . 01 49 24 04 01 . MARIONVIDAL.COM
MÉTRO ANVERS

9*th*
Map p. 272

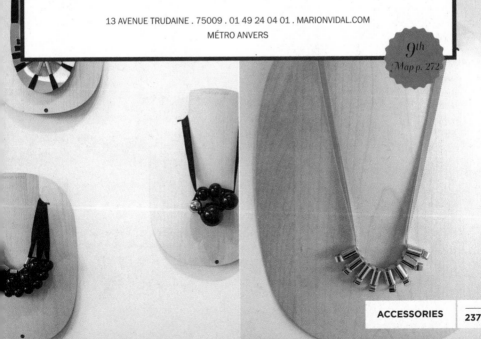

# Delphine Pariente

Previously the creator of a fine line of handbags, Delphine Pariente now applies her beautiful aesthetic to jewellery. Her style, both feminine and full of curiosities, infuses her two shops in Rue de Turenne, where old furniture is juxtaposed with the necklaces, rings and bracelets she designs and makes. You'll find an interesting collection of sign lettering, designer chairs and gorgeous carved coral flowers from old pieces that Delphine has given new life to.

8 RUE DE TURENNE . 75004 . 01 42 71 84 64 . DELPHINEPARIENTE.FR
MÉTRO SAINT-PAUL

4th
Map p. 266

feel free

# 10

## CHILDREN

Labels and websites specialising in children's fashion and lifestyle have flourished on the internet in recent years, carrying on the trend launched by the wonderful *MilK* magazine. Good shops dedicated to living spaces for children aren't so easy to find in Paris, but a few concept stores have established themselves and are now among the most innovative and envied in the world.

A duck lamp ⬡ a striped baby blanket hidden under star cushions ⬡ fairy wands that wave ⬡ a bonbon dispenser ⬡ felt mushrooms ⬡ giant floating bubbles and confetti ⬡ a red toy fox-head trophy ⬡ Chinese kites ⬡ marshmallows and lollipops

Petit Sujet Bambou Ⓛ
Balèine        18 €

# Petit Pan

The *Petit Pan* brand has several stores in Paris. The ones on Rue François Miron are the most comprehensive, with creative displays of haberdashery, fabrics by the metre, wacky kites—think flying radishes—rainbow-hued cement tiles, furniture and stationery. The hallmark of this pretty brand is its bright colours and patterns inspired by Chinese prints. They also have an online store.

37, 39 & 76 RUE FRANÇOIS MIRON . 75004 . 09 80 44 85 51 . MÉTRO SAINT-PAUL

10 RUE YVONNE LE TAC . 75018 . 01 42 23 63 78 . MÉTRO ABBESSES

95 RUE DU BAC . 75007 . 01 45 48 72 25 . MÉTRO RUE DU BAC

PETITPAN.COM

4th . 7th . 18th
Map p. 266,
p. 270 - p. 278

*If you are in Rue François Miron, have a look at number 34, where you'll find another lovely children's store:* **Mandorla Palace** *sells small furniture, decorator items and charming toys.*

# Muskhane

*Muskhane* sells felt objects made in Nepal: homewares and fashion items in a multitude of colours. It all started with the launch of a line of round rugs that were an instant hit. Initially the product colours were limited, but gradually new colours have appeared, along with new shapes and objects. There are now almost a hundred colours at *Muskhane*—showcased in seats, bins, baskets, round and rectangular rugs, mushrooms and small boats, decorative garlands, felted spheres, ottomans and pouches for phones and tablets.

3 RUE PASTOURELLE . 75003 . 09 77 06 53 47 . MUSKHANE.FR
MÉTRO SAINT-SÉBASTIEN–FROISSART

**3rd**
*Map p.264*

# Le Bonbon au Palais

This is a goldmine for those with a sweet tooth. You'll find sweets and confectionery from every region of France. Large candy jars are arranged on the main table, displaying caramels, marshmallows and lollipops in old-style wrappers. Georges, who runs the shop, sources everything directly from the confectioners and knows the history of every sweet, how and when it was made and how it got its name.

19 RUE MONGE . 75005 . 01 78 56 15 72 . BONBONSAUPALAIS.FR

MÉTRO PLACE MONGE

5*th*

*Continuing along Rue Monge, at number 47–59 you'll discover the **Arènes de Lutèce**, an amphitheatre built in the first century. It's an impressive yet peaceful spot.*

# Pain D'épices

At *Pain D'épices* you'll find a world of miniatures: fruit and vegetables carved out of wood, tiny baskets, chaises longues, electric plugs, croissants, tool boxes and furniture. The store is also known for its miniature shops with frontages that reproduce the style of old French stores. This also happens to be the only place in Paris where you'll find carded wool.

29 PASSAGE JOUFFROY . 75009 . 01 47 70 08 68 . PAINDEPICES.FR
MÉTRO RICHELIEU–DROUOT

**9**ᵗʰ
*Map p. 272*

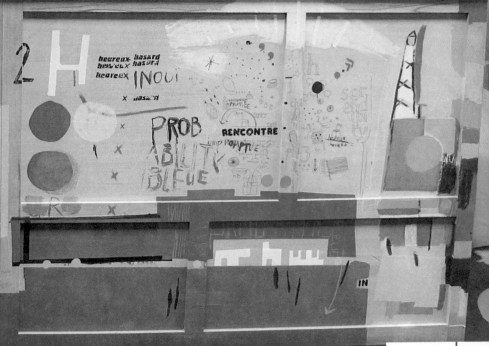

# Serendipity

This has been the leading store for interior decorating for children since 2004. Its floor space is dedicated to showcasing objects, furniture and designs. The concept of *Serendipity* is to create contemporary environments using new and vintage objects. To do this, the brand surrounds itself with young talents who sell their designs exclusively through *Serendipity*. Some products have become highly covetable, such as the skateboard shelves of *Magali Arbib* of *Leçon de choses* or the woven lamps from *Petits bohèmes*.

81–83 RUE DU CHERCHE-MIDI . 75006 . 01 40 46 01 15 . SERENDIPITY.FR
MÉTRO VANEAU

**6**<sup>th</sup>
*Map p. 268*

*You're only a few steps from* **Mamie Gâteaux,** *a perfect place for lunch and browsing through charming old pieces in the second-hand shop that's part of this restaurant and tea room.*

# Pepa's

The popular online store *Pepa's* has its Paris store in Rue des Petits Carreaux. It's in a perfect location under botanist Patrick Blanc's garden wall, *L'Oasis d'Aboukir*. You'll find 1950s-style desks from *Les Gambettes*, *Woodwork* bedside tables and *Egmont Toys* garden tables.

40 RUE DES PETITS CARREAUX . 75002 . 01 42 36 06 77 . PEPASKIDS.COM
MÉTRO SENTIER

2<sup>nd</sup>
Map p. 262

*For lunch or a good coffee, head straight to* **Frenchie to go** *on Rue du Nil, just two minutes away. For drinks or dinner, there's* **Frenchie***, the restaurant and wine bar. You might be lucky, but it's best to book ahead. 5–6 Rue du Nil . 75002 . 01 40 39 96 19*

*If you don't find what you want at Pepa's,* **Laurette** *also sells charming children's furniture and has a shop at 18 Rue Mabillon . 75006 . 01 46 34 35 22 . Métro Mabillon . LAURETTE-DECO.COM*

**CHILDREN** | 251

# Millimètres

Created in 2011 by interior decorator Laure Chédé, *Millimètres* is where you'll find designer children's furniture, shelves from the Danish brand *Gubi*, fine textile brands, such as *Brita Sweden* and *luckyboysunday*, and, more recently, clothing. It's a beautiful and meticulous collection.

19 RUE MILTON . 75009 . 01 71 70 96 99 . MILLIMETRES.FR
MÉTRO NOTRE-DAME-DE-LORETTE

9<sup>th</sup>
Map p.272

# *Bonton*

Another must-see store in Paris is *Bonton*. It was created by the Cohen family, the ingenious retail brand developers behind children's fashion store *Bonpoint*, among others. *Bonton* takes the same approach as *Bonpoint*: a spacious and elegant setting, quality selection and expertly arranged displays. With its three Paris stores, *Bonton* follows children from birth to early adolescence and sells clothing, objects and decorative accessories. You'll find a range of pretty coloured suitcases from *Ouma productions*. Highlights of the Boulevard des Filles du Calvaire store include a hairdresser, an area for birthday party accessories and a photo booth.

5 BD DES FILLES DU CALVAIRE . 75003 . 01 42 72 34 69
82 RUE DE GRENELLE . 75007 . 01 44 39 09 20
122 RUE DU BAC . 70007 . 01 42 22 77 69
BONTON.FR . MÉTRO FILLES DU CALVAIRE

3rd . 7th
Map p. 264
~ 270

**Merci** is further along the boulevard. You can have lunch there or just browse and look for inspiration. A little further again is the **Adhésifs Rubans de Normandie** store, which sells adhesive tapes in every colour: green, yellow, fluoro ... 01 42 71 31 61 . ADHESIFS.COM

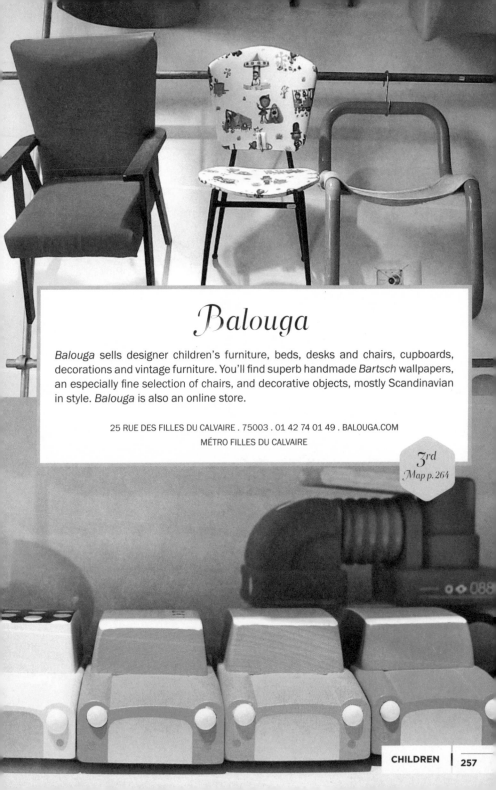

# Balouga

*Balouga* sells designer children's furniture, beds, desks and chairs, cupboards, decorations and vintage furniture. You'll find superb handmade *Bartsch* wallpapers, an especially fine selection of chairs, and decorative objects, mostly Scandinavian in style. *Balouga* is also an online store.

25 RUE DES FILLES DU CALVAIRE . 75003 . 01 42 74 01 49 . BALOUGA.COM
MÉTRO FILLES DU CALVAIRE

3rd
Map p.264

# Maps & Index

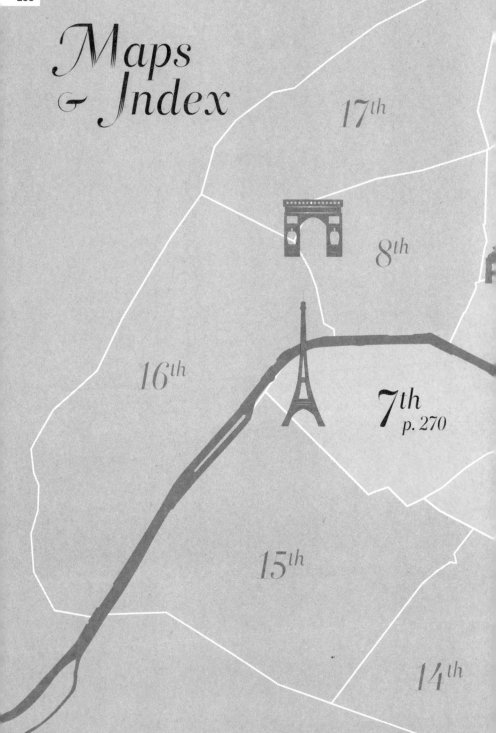

17th

8th

16th

7th
p. 270

15th

14th

**18th** p. 278

**19th**

**9th** p. 272

**10th** p. 274

**2nd** p. 262

**1st** p. 260

**3rd** p. 264

**11th** p. 276

**20th**

**6th** .268

**4th** 266

**5th**

**12th**

**13th**

# $1^{st}$ *arrondissement*

### ⬤ CONTEMPORARY INSPIRATION
1   107RIVOLI ............................ p. 34
32  Colette ................................. p. 34
7   L'Éclaireur............................ p. 89
5   Sarah Lavoine ...................... p. 34

### ⬤ TEXTILES
13  Rue Herold ........................... p. 59

### ⬤ NATURE & BOTANICALS
2   Jardin des Tuileries................ p. 74
3   Jardin des Tuileries bookstore .. p. 74
28  Odeur de Sainteté ................. p. 86
6   Stéphane Chapelle ................ p. 76
21  Vilmorin .............................. p. 93

### ⬤ VINTAGE
4   La Galcante.......................... p. 167
8   L'Oeil du Pélican .................. p. 153

### ⬤ TABLE
19  Astier de Villatte.................. p. 218
10  E. Dehillerin......................... p. 205
11  La Bovida ............................ p. 207
20  La Verrerie des Halles .......... p. 205
12  Mora .................................. p. 207
15  Tsé & Tsé ............................ p. 213
14  Zero One One...................... p. 210

### ⬤ ACCESSORIES
16  Journal Standard de Luxe ... p. 226
17  La Droguerie de Paris........... p. 225
18  Mokuba .............................. p. 232

### FOOD & DRINK
25  Angelina .............................. p. 20
34  Café Le Nemours................... p. 25
30  Café Verlet........................... p. 25
9   Claus .................................. p. 153
27  Coutume Lab ....................... p. 25
33  Izakaya Issé.......................... p. 76
23  Jean-Paul Hévin .................... p. 20
22  Kunitoraya ............................ p. 19
35  La Régalade Saint-Honoré.......p. 13
24  Le Garde Robe ...................... p. 23
31  Télescope ............................ p. 25
26  Verjus.................................. p. 23

 Café     Restaurant

🍺 Bar     Market    H Hotel

2nd
p. 262

6th
p. 268

# $2^{nd}$ *arrondissement*

**CONTEMPORARY INSPIRATION**
3  Persona Grata............................p. 46

**TEXTILES**
4  C M O....................................p. 57

**NATURE & BOTANICALS**
19  Design et Nature........................p. 84
14  Hervé Châtelain.........................p. 77

**ART & COLOUR**
17  Lavrut ....................................p. 102
11  Legeron ..................................p. 109
16  RD Spectacles...........................p. 109

**VINTAGE**
1  Kidimo...................................p. 150

**WORLD DÉCOR**
20  The Appointment ...................p. 190
6  Rickshaw.................................p. 192

**TABLE**
5  A. Simon .................................p. 207
2  G. Detou .................................p. 206

**ACCESSORIES**
9  En Selle Marcel.......................p. 229
12  Kiliwatch................................p. 229
8  Pour Vos Beaux Yeux...............p. 227
18  Shindo ...................................p. 233
10  Ultramod ...............................p. 224

**CHILDREN**
13  Pepa's...................................p. 251

**FOOD & DRINK**
15  Coinstot Vino..........................p. 19
25  Experimental Cocktail Club......p. 23
23  Frenchie.................................p. 251
21  Racines..................................p. 77
24  Terroirs d'Avenir....................p. 27

 Café   Restaurant
 Bar  Market  H Hotel

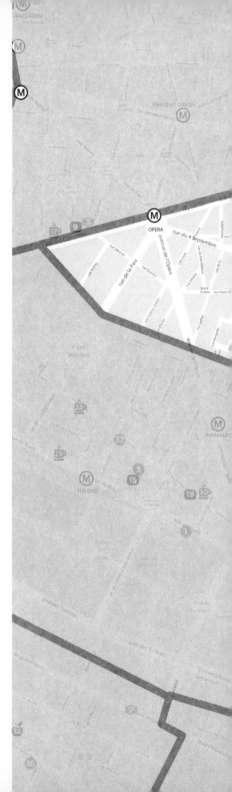

# $3^{rd}$ *arrondissement*

● **CONTEMPORARY INSPIRATION**
1  Gallery S. Bensimon ................. p. 45
2  Home Autour du Monde ........... p. 45
9  Marcel By ................................ p. 41
23  Mona Market............................ p. 47
33  Papier Tigre ............................ p. 43
8  The Collection .......................... p. 51

● **NATURE & BOTANICALS**
24  Galerie Chardon........................ p. 84
4  Jardin du Musée Carnavalet ..... p. 74
36  Jardin Saint-Gilles-Grand-Veneur.. p. 74

⬡ **TOOL BOX**
35  Adhésifs Rubans de Normandie p. 255
18  Tartaix .................................... p. 121
16/17 Weber.................................... p. 123

◗ **VINTAGE**
10  Galerie Et Caetera .................. p. 143
37  Impossible ............................... p. 231
5  Jérôme Lepert .......................... p. 151
3  Pep's........................................ p. 150

◗ **WORLD DÉCOR**
14  CSAO ......................................p. 189

▪ **TABLE**
12  Merci........................................ p. 203
20  UP ........................................... p. 210

● **ACCESSORIES**
7  Isaac Reina .............................p. 236
13  Khadi and Co ..........................p. 235
19  Yves Andrieux & Vincent Jalbert p. 231

⬡ **CHILDREN**
31  Balouga .................................... p. 257
21  Bonton ..................................... p. 255
15  Muskhane ................................ p. 245

**FOOD & DRINK**
11  Blend ....................................... p. 203
39  Boot Café ................................ p. 25
26  Chez Nénesse........................... p. 19
30  Fondation Café ........................ p. 25
38  Fragments................................ p. 25
29  Le Loustic ............................... p. 25
22  Le Mary Céleste ...................... p. 47
32  Marché Couvert des Enfants Rouges p. 26
34  Popelini.................................... p. 21
6  The Broken Arm ....................... p. 25
28  The Little Red Door.................. p. 23

**HOTELS**
25  Hôtel Jules et Jim..................... p. 17

☕ Café    🍴 Restaurant

🍹 Bar    🍎 Market    **H** Hotel

## 10th
p. 274

## 11th
p. 276

## 4th
p. 266

# $4^{th}$ *arrondissement*

● **CONTEMPORARY INSPIRATION**
8  FR 66.............................................p. 41
27  Galeries Sentou ........................ p. 40
7  Portobello..................................p. 36

◗ **TEXTILES**
22  Caravane ................................... p. 56
23  Kilim Ada ...................................p. 61

● **NATURE & BOTANICALS**
2  Bibliothèque Forney.................p. 74
5  Marché aux Fleurs et aux Oiseaux.. p. 93
9  Miller et Bertaux .......................p. 87

⬢ **ART & COLOUR**
16  Calligrane ............................... p. 100
14  La Maison du Pastel .............. p. 99
15  Papier Plus ............................ p. 101

⬡ **TOOL BOX**
25  BHV .......................................... p. 100
1  The Little Shop of Colours.... p. 129

⬟ **VINTAGE**
4  Au Bon Usage....................... p. 210
10  Au Petit Bonheur la Chance .. p. 155

🛡 **WORLD DÉCOR**
24  C&P............................................ p. 191
12  La Cabane de l'Ours............. p. 193

■ **TABLE**
29  Argenterie d'Antan................. p. 212
11  Corner Shop ............................ p. 210
17  Fleux ........................................ p. 217

● **ACCESSORIES**
28  Delphine Pariente................. p. 239

⬡ **CHILDREN**
6  Mandorla Palace.................... p. 244
18  Petit Pan .................................. p. 244

**FOOD & DRINK**
31  Berthillon.................................. p. 20
20  Florence Kahn..........................p. 87
26  Izraël......................................... p. 40
32  La Caféothèque ...................... p. 25
21  L'As du Fallafel........................p. 87
3  Le Sergent Recruteur ............. p. 19
30  Loir dans la Théière................ p. 20
34  Mon Vieil Ami ......................... p. 13
13  Pain de Sucre........................... p. 99
19  Sacha Finkelsztajn .................p. 87

☕ Café  🍴 Restaurant  🍺 Bar  🍎 Market  H Hotel

3rd
p. 264

# $6^{th}$ *arrondissement*

**CONTEMPORARY INSPIRATION**
24  Catherine Memmi..................p. 91

**TEXTILES**
12  Adèle Shaw.............................. p. 65
18  Caravane La Maison.............. p. 56
14  Secret Maison.........................p. 91

**NATURE & BOTANICALS**
3   Cire Trudon.............................p. 91
21  Hermès..................................... p. 85
20  Jardin du Luxembourg............p. 74
4   Odorantes.................................. p. 78

**ART & COLOUR**
13  La Compagnie du Kraft........ p. 104

**VINTAGE**
17  La Galerie Salon ................... p. 166
2   Librairie Alain Brieux  ........... p. 168
6   Marion Held Javal ................. p. 162
5   Yveline ..................................... p. 163

**TABLE**
7   Ceccaldi................................... p. 209
8   Xanadou ................................. p. 210

**ACCESSORIES**
15  Ralph Lauren Vintage........... p. 229

**CHILDREN**
1   Laurette.................................. p. 251
19  Serendipity............................. p. 250

**FOOD & DRINK**
9   La Crèmerie............................. p. 19
10  L'Avant Comptoir..................... p. 23
23  Le Bar du Marché.................. p. 25
25  Le Marché Raspail...................p. 27
16  Mamie Gâteaux ..................... p. 250
22  Pierre Hermé...........................p. 21

 Café   Restaurant
 Bar   Market   Hotel

$7^{th}$ *p. 270*

# $7^{th}$ *arrondissement*

**CONTEMPORARY INSPIRATION**
17  Galeries Sentou ..................p. 40
2   India Mahdavi ......................p. 49
9   Le Bon Marché..................p. 85
10  Maison M .............................p. 43
16  Sarah Lavoine ......................p. 34

**TEXTILES**
8   La Soie Disante....................p. 67

**NATURE & BOTANICALS**
5   Deyrolle...............................p. 84
18  Flower .................................p. 79

**ART & COLOUR**
7   Sennelier ............................ p. 104

**VINTAGE**
11  Librairie Elbé ...................... p. 169

**WORLD DÉCOR**
1   CFOC...................................p. 195

**CHILDREN**
3   Bonton ................................ p. 255
4   Bonton ................................ p. 255
6   Petit Pan ............................. p. 244

**FOOD & DRINK**
15  Coutume Café ......................p. 25
14  La Grande Épicerie de Paris p. 85
12  L'Épicerie Générale...............p. 79
13  Merveilleux...........................p. 21

 Café    Restaurant

 Bar    Market    Hotel

quai d'Orsay

port des Invalides

quai d'Orsay

**M** quai d'Orsay
**INVALIDES**

Gare des
Invalides

quai Anatole France

quai de Solférino

port de Solférino

quai Anatole France

bd St-Germain

rue de Lille

**M** **INVALIDES**

**ASSEMBLEE NATIONALE**

rue de l'Université

rue de Lille

rue de l'Université

quai Anatole France

**MUSEE D'ORSAY**

place
Henry
de
Montherlant

rue de Bellechasse

rue de Poitiers

rue de Lille

Pont
Royal

**M** quai Anatole France

rue de l'Université

rue du Bac

**7** Quai Voltaire

rue de Constantine

rue Eblé

rue Saint-Dominique

place du
Palais
Bourbon

rue de l'Université

rue Las Cases

**1**

**M** **SOLFERINO**

boulevard Saint-Germain

rue de l'Exposition

**12**

rue de l'Université

rue de Lille

**8**

rue de Verneuil

**18**

rue de Grenelle

**10**

rue de Bourgogne

rue de Martignac

rue Casimir-Périer

**2**

**2**

rue Saint-Dominique

rue de Bourgogne

rue de Champagny

Mairie

rue de Grenelle

rue Saint-Guillaume

rue de Bellechasse

**16**

rue de Sèvres

rue Montalembert

bd des Invalides

**M** **VARENNE**

rue de Varenne

rue de Bourgogne

rue de Varenne

rue Barbet-de-Jouy

rue Vaneau

place de la
Visitation

rue de Luynes

rue Paul-Louis Courier

**11**

rue de Grenelle

**5**

rue Perronet

rue du Pré aux Clercs

place
Jacques
Copeau

**RUE DU BAC**

**M**

**3**

boulevard Raspail

bld St-Germain

rue du Bac

rue de Saint-Simon

rue de Bellechasse

bld St-Germain

rue du Cherche-Midi

bd des Invalides

rue de Varenne

rue de Sèvres

rue de Verneuil

rue de Luynes

rue de Grenelle

rue Chomel

rue de Babylone

rue Récamier

sq. Chose
Récamier

**15**

rue Rousselet

rue Oudinot

rue Rousselet

rue Chanaleilles

rue Vaneau

rue de Sèvres

**6**

square de
La Rochefoucauld

rue de Babylone

rue de Commaille

boulevard Raspail

**17**

rue de Luynes

rue Masseran

sq. des Missions
Etrangères

**4**

rue de Babylone

**SEVRES BABYLONE**

rue Monsieur

**M**

bd des Invalides

**M** **SAINT FRANCOIS XAVIER**

place
Amélie

rue de Babylone

**15**

rue Rousselet

rue Oudinot

rue Rousselet

rue Oudinot

rue d'Olivet

rue Mayet

rue Dupin

**14** **9**

**21**

**M** **SAINT SULPICE**

**4**

rue Chomel

bd des Invalides

rue Rousselet

rue de Sèvres

rue Mayet

**M**
VANEAU

**19**

**10**
**11**

**6**th
p. 268

**25**

**M**
**SÈVRES**

**SAINT ROCH**

**M**

**M** **DUROC**

# $9^{th}$ *arrondissement*

**NATURE & BOTANICALS**
24  Musée de la Vie Romantique ...... p. 75

**ART & COLOUR**
5  Talents ................................ p. 115
1  The Drawer ........................... p. 165

**TOOL BOX**
4  Vincent Guerre ...................... p. 136

**VINTAGE**
3  Antiquitiés Arthur Bruet ........ p. 161
2  Dank .................................... p. 165
7  Phonogalerie ........................ p. 159

**TABLE**
23  À Ma Table ........................... p. 215
9  Perigot ................................. p. 211

**ACCESSORIES**
8  Marion Vidal ......................... p. 237

**CHILDREN**
10  Millimètres ........................... p. 253
11  Pain D'épices ........................ p. 247

**FOOD & DRINK**
19  Artisan ................................. p. 23
27  Café Marlette ........................ p. 159
13  Caillebotte ............................ p. 19
21  Coffélia ................................ p. 25
22  Glass ................................... p. 23
14  KB ....................................... p. 25
20  La Chambre aux Confitures .... p. 21
17  La Maison du Chocolat .......... p. 21
25  Le Marché d'Anvers ............... p. 26
26  Les Commis .......................... p. 215
16  Popelini ................................ p. 21
18  Sébastien Gaudard ................ p. 20

**HOTELS**
15  Hôtel de Nell ........................ p. 17
12  Hôtel du Temps ..................... p. 17

 Café    Restaurant

 Bar    Market    Hotel

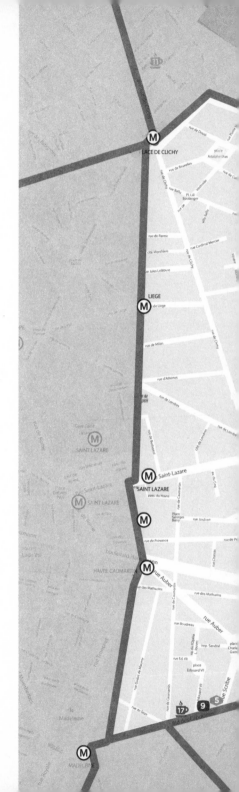

# 18th
## p. 278

BLANCHE

PIGALLE

ANVERS

place
d'Anvers **25**

avenue Trudaine **8**

**22**

**7**

**24**

**23** ue Trudaine

**19**
**14** **26** **2**
**1**

**27** **21**

**16**

SAINT GEORGES

**10**

**18**

**20**

**3**

**13**

N.D DE LORETTE

TRINITE

CADET

POISSONNIERE

H **12**

H **15**

LE PELETIER

**4**

CHAUSSEE D'ANTIN

boulevard Haussmann

**11**

**16**
**3**

RICHELIEU
DROUOT

GRANDS
BOULEVARDS

BONNE NOUVELLE

**21**
**15**

# 2nd
## p. 262

**10**

BOURSE

# $10^{th}$ *arrondissement*

### ● CONTEMPORARY INSPIRATION
4   Artazart.....................................p. 45
1   Colonel.....................................p. 37
2   Kann Design.............................p. 35

### ● ART & COLOUR
15  Cristalleries Schweitzer ......p. 107
8   Cuirs Chadefaux................. p. 110
11  Emmanuelle Wittmann...... p. 114

### ● TOOL BOX
20  Le Comptoir Alexandre ...... p. 126

### ● VINTAGE
7   Broc Martel.......................... p. 158
28  No Factory ........................... p. 145
9   Objet Céleste....................... p. 145

### ● WORLD DÉCOR
31  Jamini ................................. p. 187
5   Le Comptoir Général.......... p. 188

### ● TABLE
14  La Cristallerie de Paris .......p. 216
13  La Maison de la Porcelaine..p. 216
32  La Trésorerie ....................... p. 219

### ● ACCESSORIES
10  Jean-Marc Poursin .................p. 35
30  Le Centre Commercial..........p. 13

### ● CHILDREN
25  La Piñata ...............................p. 35

### FOOD & DRINK
17  Bar Le Coq.............................p. 23
29  Bob's Juice Bar .....................p. 13
22  Café Craft ..............................p. 25
23  Du Pain et Des Idées......... p. 145
6   Helmut Newcake....................p. 20
24  Holybelly ...............................p. 25
27  Le Fantôme ...........................p. 12
16  Le Richer ...............................p. 19
19  Loft Design By .......................p. 35
26  Sol Semilla ............................p. 35
18  Ten Belles .............................p. 25
21  Tuck Shop..............................p. 25

### HOTELS
3   Hôtel Paradis........................p. 17

 Café    Restaurant

 Bar    Market   H Hotel

# $2nd$
*p. 262*

# 11<sup>th</sup> arrondissement

## TEXTILES
8    Lindell and Co .......................... p. 63

## ART & COLOUR
18    Cannage-Paillage................. p. 136
7    Patricia Vieljeux .................. p. 112
5    Peausserie Poulain............ p. 111

## TOOL BOX
13    Au Progrès ........................... p. 124
9    Emery & Cie ........................ p. 128
6    Le Petit FabLab.................. p. 123

## VINTAGE
1    Anna Colore......................... p. 154

## WORLD DÉCOR
22    Mahatsara............................ p. 196
4    Ouma Productions.............. p. 197

## FOOD & DRINK
20    Aux Deux Amis ...................... p. 23
12    Bistrot Paul Bert................... p. 124
17    Bones .................................... p. 23
3    Caffè dei Cioppi ..................... p. 19
21    La Manufacture Alain Ducasse ..p. 21
10    La Pâtisserie Cyril Lignac .. p. 124
14    L'Entrée des Artistes............. p. 23
19    Le Perchoir .......................... p. 190
11    Le Pure Café........................ p. 124
15    Septime ................................ p. 19

 Café     Restaurant

 Bar     Market     Hotel

MÉNILMONTANT **M**

**6**

**19**

PARMENTIER **M**
de la République

RUE ST MAUR **M**
av. de la République

PÈRE LACHAISE **M**

SAINT AMBROISE **M**

square
Maurice
Gardette

square
Marcel Rajman

bld Voltaire

Mairie

bld Voltaire

place
Léon Blum

VOLTAIRE **M**

PHILIPPE AUGUSTE **M**

place
du Père
Chaillet

**17**

bld Voltaire

**7**

CHARONNE **M**
bld Voltaire

rue de Charonne

**15**

**11**

**18**

**10**

RUE DES BOULETS **M**
bld Volt.

**9**

rue de Chanzy

**12**

LEDRU ROLLIN **M**

**3**

**13**

**1**

**M**

FAIDHERBE CHALIGNY

# $18^{th}$ *arrondissement*

**CONTEMPORARY INSPIRATION**
4    Les Peintures XVIIIᵉ..............p. 80

**TEXTILES**
8    Dreyfus ....................................p. 69
5    Marché Saint-Pierre..............p. 69
9    Tissus Reine...........................p. 69
12   Sacrés Coupons....................p. 69

**NATURE & BOTANICALS**
3    Les Mauvaises Graines........p. 80

**VINTAGE**
1    Tombées du Camion............p. 147
2    Zut!......................................... p. 144

**CHILDREN**
7    Petit Pan............................. p. 244

**FOOD & DRINK**
6    Café Lomi ...............................p. 25
11   Le Bal Café.............................p. 25

**HOTELS**
10   L'Hôtel Particulier.................p. 75

 Café   Restaurant
 Bar   Market   Hotel

**107RIVOLI** . . . . . . . . . . . . 34
107 rue de Rivoli . 75001
01 42 60 64 94
lesartsdecoratifs.fr

# A

**À L'ÉPI D'OR** . . . . . . . . . 127
17 rue des Bernardins . 75005
01 46 33 17 16
salledebain-epidor.com

**À MA TABLE** . . . . . . . . . . 215
72 rue des Martyrs . 75009
09 67 40 49 31 . a-ma-table.fr

**A. SIMON** . . . . . . . . . . . . 207
48-52 rue Montmartre . 75002
01 42 33 71 65

**ADAM** . . . . . . . . . . . . . . 102
11 bd Edgar Quinet . 75014
01 43 20 68 53

**ADÈLE SHAW** . . . . . . . . . 65
33 rue Jacob . 75006
01 42 60 80 72

**ADHÉSIFS RUBANS
DE NORMANDIE** . . . . . . . 255
93 bd Beaumarchais . 75003
01 42 71 31 61 . adhesifs.com

**ANGELINA** . . . . . . . . . . . . 20
226 rue de Rivoli . 75001
01 42 60 82 00
angelina-paris.fr

**ANNA COLORE** . . . . . . . . 154
7 rue Paul Bert . 75011
01 43 79 41 62
anna-colore-industriale.com

**ANTIQUITIÉS
ARTHUR BRUET** . . . . . . . .161
30 rue Saint-Lazare . 75009
06 13 23 74 17

**THE APPOINTMENT** . . . . 190
14 rue Beauregard . 75002

**ARÈNES DE LUTÈCE** . . . . . 75
59 rue Monge . 75005
01 45 35 02 56

**ARGENTERIE D'ANTAN** . . 212
6 rue de Birague . 75004
01 42 71 31 91
argenterie-dantan.com

**ARTAZART** . . . . . . . . . . . . 45
83 quai de Valmy . 75010
01 40 40 24 00 . artazart.com

**ARTISAN** . . . . . . . . . . . . . 23
14 rue Bochart de Saron . 75009
01 48 74 65 38 . artisan-bar.com

**L'AS DU FALLAFEL** . . . . . . 87
34 rue des Rosiers . 75004
01 48 87 63 60

**ASTIER DE VILLATTE** . . . 218
173 rue Saint-Honoré . 75001
01 42 60 74 13
astierdevillatte.com

**L'ATELIER DU CUIVRE** . . 137
111 avenue Daumesnil . 75012
01 43 40 20 20

**ATELIER GARNERO** . . . . 137
46 bd Brune . 75014
01 45 43 70 08

**AU BON USAGE** . . . . . . . 210
21 rue Saint-Paul . 75004
01 42 78 80 14
aubonusage.com

**AU PETIT BONHEUR
LA CHANCE** . . . . . . . . . . 155
13 rue Saint-Paul . 75004
01 42 74 36 38

**AU PROGRÈS** . . . . . . . . . 124
11 bis rue Faidherbe Chaligny
75011 . 01 43 71 70 61
auprogres.com

**AUX DEUX AMIS** . . . . . . . 23
45 rue Oberkampf . 75011
01 58 30 38 13

**L'AVANT COMPTOIR** . . . . . 23
3 carrefour de l'Odéon . 75006
01 44 27 07 97

# B

**BAAN** . . . . . . . . . . . . . . . 187
13 rue de la Revolution
94200 Ivry-sur-Seine
06 23 46 09 61 . baan-baan.com

**BACHELIER** . . . . . . . . . . 180
Puces de St-Ouen, Marché Paul Bert
Allée 1, stand 17
01 40 11 89 98
bachelier-antiquites.com

**LE BAL CAFÉ** . . . . . . . . . . 25
6 impasse de la Défense . 75018
01 44 70 75 51 . le-bal.fr

**BALOUGA** . . . . . . . . . . . . 257
25 rue des Filles-du-Calvaire
75003 . 01 42 74 01 49
balouga.com

**LE BAR DU MARCHÉ** . . . . . 25
75 rue de Seine . 75006
01 43 26 55 15

**BAR LE COQ** . . . . . . . . . . 23
12 rue du Château d'eau . 75010
01 42 40 85 68

**BENNETON GRAVEUR** . . 103
75 boulevard Malesherbes . 75008
01 43 87 57 39
boutique.bennetongraveur.com

**BERTHILLON** . . . . . . . . . . 20
31 rue Saint-Louis-en-l'Île . 75004
01 43 54 31 61
berthillon.fr

**BHV** . . . . . . . . . . . . . . . . 100
34 rue de la Verrerie . 75004
09 77 40 14 00
bhv.fr

**BIBLIOTHÈQUE FORNEY** . . 74
1 rue du Figuier . 75004
01 42 78 14 60

**BISTROT PAUL BERT** . . . 124
18 rue Paul Bert . 75011
01 43 72 24 01

**BLEND** . . . . . . . . . . . . . . 203
1 bd des Filles du Calvaire . 75003
blendhamburger.com

**BOB'S JUICE BAR** . . . . . . . 13
15 rue Lucien Sampaix . 75010
09 50 06 36 18
bobsjuicebar.com

**LE BON MARCHÉ** . . . . . . . 85
24 rue de Sèvres . 75006
01 44 39 80 00
lebonmarche.com

**LE BONBON AU PALAIS** . . 246
19 rue Monge . 75005
01 78 56 15 72
bonbonsaupalais.fr

**BONES** . . . . . . . . . . . . . . 23
43 rue Godefroy Cavaignac . 75011
09 80 75 32 08
bonesparis.com

**BONTON** . . . . . . . . . . . . . **255**
5 boulevard des Filles-du-Calvaire
75003 . 01 42 72 34 69
82 rue de Grenelle . 75007
01 44 39 09 20
122 rue du Bac . 75007
01 42 22 77 69
bonton.fr

**BOOT CAFÉ** . . . . . . . . . . . **25**
19 rue du Pont-aux-Choux . 75003
01 73 70 14 57
lebootcafe.fr

**LA BOVIDA** . . . . . . . . . . . **207**
36 rue Montmartre . 75001
01 42 36 09 99
labovida.com

**BROC MARTEL** . . . . . . . . **158**
12 rue Martel . 75010
01 48 24 53 43
brocmartel.com

**THE BROKEN ARM** . . . . . . **25**
12 rue Perrée . 75003
01 44 61 53 60
the-broken-arm.com

**BRÛLERIE
DE BELLEVILLE** . . . . . . . . **25**
10 rue de Pradier . 75019
09 83 75 60 80
cafesbelleville.com

*C*

**C&P** . . . . . . . . . . . . . . . . . . **191**
16 rue du Pont Louis-Philippe
75004 . 01 42 74 22 34

**LA CABANE DE L'OURS** . . **193**
23 rue Saint-Paul . 75004
01 42 71 01 49
lacabanedelours.com

**CAFÉ CRAFT** . . . . . . . . . . **25**
24 rue des Vinaigriers . 75010
01 40 35 90 77
café-craft.com

**CAFÉ LE NEMOURS** . . . . . **25**
2 place Colette . 75001
01 42 61 34 14

**CAFÉ LOMI** . . . . . . . . . . . **25**
3 ter rue Marcadet . 75018
09 80 39 56 24
cafelomi.com

**CAFÉ MARLETTE** . . . . . . **159**
51 rue des Martyrs . 75009
marlettegourmet.blogspot.com

**CAFÉ VERLET** . . . . . . . . . **25**
256 rue Saint-Honoré . 75001
01 42 60 67 39
verlet.fr

**LA CAFÉOTHÈQUE** . . . . . . **25**
52 rue de l'Hôtel de Ville . 75004
01 53 01 83 84
lacafeotheque.com

**CAFFÈ DEI CIOPPI** . . . . . . **19**
159 rue du Faubourg Saint-Antoine
75011 . 01 43 46 10 14

**CAILLEBOTTE** . . . . . . . . . . **18**
8 rue Hippolyte Lebas . 75009
01 53 20 88 70

**CALLIGRANE** . . . . . . . . . . **100**
6 rue du Pont Louis-Philippe
75004 . 01 48 04 09 00
calligrane.fr

**CANNAGE-PAILLAGE** . . . **136**
58 rue de Charonne . 75011
01 48 05 29 40

**CARAVANE** . . . . . . . . . . . . **56**
6 rue Pavée . 75004
01 44 51 04 20
caravane.fr
    **CHAMBRE 19** . . . . . . . . **56**
    19 rue Saint-Nicolas . 75012
    01 44 61 04 20
    **EMPORIUM** . . . . . . . . . **214**
    22 rue Saint-Nicolas . 75012
    01 53 17 18 55
    **LA MAISON** . . . . . . . . . **56**
    9 rue Jacob . 75006
    01 53 10 08 86

**CARRELAGES DES SUDS** . . **131**
24 boulevard Saint-Germain
75005 . 01 40 51 01 01

**CATHERINE MEMMI** . . . . . . **91**
11 rue Saint-Sulpice
75006 . 01 44 07 02 02
catherinememmi.com

**CECCALDI** . . . . . . . . . . . . **209**
15 rue Racine . 75006
01 46 33 87 20
couteaux-ceccaldi.com

**LE CENTRE COMMERCIAL** . **13**
2 rue de Marseille . 75010
01 42 02 26 08
centrecommercial.cc

**CFOC** . . . . . . . . . . . . . . . **195**
260 bd Saint-Germain . 75007
01 47 05 92 82
170 bd Hausmann . 75008
01 53 53 40 80
cfoc.fr

**LA CHAMBRE AUX
CONFITURES** . . . . . . . . . . **21**
9 rue des Martyrs . 75009
01 71 73 43 77
lachambreauxconfitures.com

**CHARBONNEL** . . . . . . . . **103**
13 quai Montebello . 75005
01 43 54 23 46

**CHEZ NÉNESSE** . . . . . . . . **19**
17 rue de Saintonge . 75003
01 42 78 46 49

**CIRE TRUDON** . . . . . . . . . **91**
78 rue de Seine . 75006
01 43 26 46 50
ciretrudon.com

**CLAUDE NATURE** . . . . . . . **81**
32 bd Saint-Germain . 75005
01 44 07 30 79
claudenature.com

**CLAUS** . . . . . . . . . . . . . . . **153**
14 rue Jean-Jacques Rousseau
75001 . 01 42 33 55 10
clausparis.com

**CMO** . . . . . . . . . . . . . . . . . **57**
5 rue Chabanais . 75002
01 40 20 45 98
cmoparis.com

**COFFÉLIA** . . . . . . . . . . . . **25**
45 rue Condorcet . 75009
01 40 16 04 68
coffelia.fr

**COINSTOT VINO** . . . . . . . . **19**
26 bis passage des Panoramas
75002 . 01 44 82 08 54
coinstot-vino.com

**COLETTE** . . . . . . . . . . . . . **34**
213 rue Saint-Honoré . 75001
01 55 35 33 90 . colette.fr

**THE COLLECTION** . . . . . . . **51**
33 rue de Poitou . 75003
01 42 77 04 20
the-collection.fr

**COLONEL** . . . . . . . . . . . . . **37**
14 avenue Richerand . 75010
01 83 89 69 22 . moncolonel.fr

**COLONIAL CONCEPT . . . 177**
Puces de St-Ouen, 8 rue Paul Bert
01 40 10 00 71
francoisdaneck.com

**LES COMMIS . . . . . . . . . 215**
51 avenue Trudaine . 75009
01 48 74 83 14
lescommis.com

**LA COMPAGNIE
DU KRAFT . . . . . . . . . . . 104**
12 rue Jacob . 75006
01 46 34 38 48 . lekraft.com

**LE COMPTOIR
ALEXANDRE . . . . . . . . . 126**
58 rue de Paradis . 75010
01 48 24 67 36
comptoiralexandre.com

**LE COMPTOIR GÉNÉRAL . 188**
80 quai de Jemmapes . 75010
01 44 88 20 45
lecomptoirgeneral.com

**CORNER SHOP . . . . . . . 210**
3 rue Saint-Paul . 75004
01 42 77 50 88

**COUTUME CAFÉ . . . . . . . 25**
47 rue de Babylone . 75007
01 45 51 50 47
coutumecafe.com

**COUTUME LAB . . . . . . . . 25**
4 rue du Bouloi . 75001
01 45 51 50 47

**LA CRÈMERIE . . . . . . . . . 19**
9 rue des Quatre-Vents . 75006
01 43 54 99 30
lacremerie.fr

**LA CRISTALLERIE
DE PARIS . . . . . . . . . . . . 216**
1 rue de Paradis . 75010
01 47 70 20 54
cristallerie-de-paris.fr

**CRISTALLERIES
SCHWEITZER. . . . . . . . . 107**
84 quai de Jemmapes . 75010
01 42 39 61 63
cristalleries-schweitzer.fr

**CSAO . . . . . . . . . . . . . . . 189**
9 rue Elzévir . 75003
01 42 71 33 17 . csao.fr

**CUIRS CHADEFAUX . . . . 110**
18 rue Taylor . 75010
01 42 08 18 61
cuirschadefaux.com

# D

**DANK . . . . . . . . . . . . . . . 165**
8 rue Bochart de Saron . 75009
06 74 58 11 91 . dank.fr

**DELPHINE PARIENTE . . . 239**
8 rue de Turenne . 75004
01 42 71 84 64
delphinepariente.fr

**DESIGN ET NATURE . . . . . 84**
4 rue d'Aboukir . 75002
01 43 06 86 98
designetnature.fr

**DEYROLLE . . . . . . . . . . . . 84**
46 rue du Bac . 75007
01 42 22 30 07 . deyrolle.fr

**DIPTYQUE . . . . . . . . . . . . 90**
34 bd Saint-Germain . 75005
01 43 26 77 44
diptyqueparis.fr

**THE DRAWER . . . . . . . . . 165**
6 rue Bochart de Saron . 75009
thedrawer.net

**DREYFUS . . . . . . . . . . . . . 69**
2 rue Charles Nodier . 75018
01 46 06 92 25

**LA DROGUERIE . . . . . . . 225**
9 & 11 rue du Jour . 75001
01 45 08 93 27
ladroguerie.com

**DUBOIS. . . . . . . . . . . . . . 105**
20 rue Soufflot . 75005
01 44 41 67 50 . dubois-paris.com

**DUGAY . . . . . . . . . . . . . . 175**
Puces de St-Ouen, 92 rue des Rosiers
01 40 11 87 30
produits-dugay.com

**THE DUKE . . . . . . . . . . . 179**
Puces de St-Ouen, Marché Vernaison
99 rue des Rosiers
Allée 1, Shop 37
06 32 37 17 11

**DU PAIN ET DES IDÉES . 145**
34 rue Yves Toudic . 75010
01 42 40 44 52
dupainetdesidees.com

# E

**E. DEHILLERIN. . . . . . . . 205**
18-20 rue Coquillière . 75001
01 42 36 53 13
e-dehillerin.fr

**L'ÉBAUCHOIR . . . . . . . . . 19**
43–45 rue de Citeaux . 75012
01 43 42 49 31
lebauchoir.com

**L'ÉCLAIREUR. . . . . . . . . . 89**
10 rue Hérold . 75001
01 40 41 09 89
leclaireur.com

**ELODIE SANSON. . . . . . . 179**
Puces de St-Ouen
Marché Vernaison
Allée 2, Stand 51 bis
06 10 01 38 97

**EMERY & CIE . . . . . . . . . 128**
18 passage de la Main d'or
75011
emeryetcie.com

**EMMANUELLE
WITTMANN. . . . . . . . . . . . 114**
13 rue des Récollets . 75010
01 43 80 01 24

**EN SELLE MARCEL . . . . . 229**
40 rue Tiquetonne . 75002
01 44 54 06 46
ensellemarcel.com

**L'ENTRÉE DES ARTISTES. . 23**
8 rue de Crossol . 75011
09 50 99 67 11

**L'ÉPICERIE GÉNÉRALE. . . 79**
43 rue de Verneuil . 75007
01 42 60 51 78
epiceriegenerale.fr

**ESPACE CULTUREL
LOUIS VUITTON. . . . . . . . 195**
60 rue de Bassano . 75008
01 45 06 26 94
louisvuitton-espaceculturel.com

**EXPERIMENTAL
COCKTAIL CLUB . . . . . . . . 23**
37 rue Saint-Sauveur . 75002
01 45 08 88 09
experimentalcocktailbar.fr

# F

**FANETTE** . . . . . . . . . . . . 153
1 rue d'Alençon . 75015

**LE FANTÔME** . . . . . . . . . . 12
36 rue de Paradis . 75010
09 66 87 11 20

**FLEUX** . . . . . . . . . . . . . . . 217
39 & 52 rue Sainte-Croix de la
Bretonnerie . 75004
01 42 78 27 20
fleux.com

**FLORENCE KAHN** . . . . . . . 87
24 rue des Écouffes . 75004
01 48 87 92 85
florence-kahn.fr

**FLOWER** . . . . . . . . . . . . . . 79
14 rue des Saints-Pères . 75007
01 44 50 00 20
flower.fr

**FONDATION CAFÉ** . . . . . . 25
16 rue Dupetit-Thouars . 75003
fondationcafe.com

**FR 66** . . . . . . . . . . . . . . . 41
25 rue du Renard . 75004
01 44 54 35 36 . fr66.com

**FRAGMENTS** . . . . . . . . . . 25
76 rue des Tournelles . 75003

**FRENCHIE** . . . . . . . . . . . 251
5–6 rue du Nil . 75002
01 40 39 96 19
frenchie-restaurant.com

**FRENCHIE TO GO** . . . . . . . 27
9 rue du Nil . 75002
01 40 39 96 19
frenchietogo.com

# G

**G. DETOU** . . . . . . . . . . . . 206
58 rue Tiquetonne . 75002
01 42 36 54 67
gdetou.com

**LA GALCANTE** . . . . . . . . 167
52 rue de l'Arbre Sec . 75001
01 44 77 87 44
lagalcante.com

**GALERIE CHARDON** . . . . . 84
21-23 rue des Filles-du-Calvaire
75003 . 01 42 74 58 10
galerie-chardon.fr

**GALERIE ET CAETERA** . . 143
40 rue de Poitou . 75003
06 66 92 75 77
franckdelmarcelle.com

**LA GALERIE SALON** . . . . 166
4 rue Bourbon-le-Château
75006 . 06 33 85 98 99
galeriesalon.blogspot.com

**GALERIES SENTOU** . . . . . .40
26 bd Raspail . 75007
01 45 49 00 05
29 rue François Miron . 75004
01 42 78 50 60
112 bd de Courcelles . 75017
01 82 83 52 90
sentou.fr

**GALERIE URUBAMBA** . . . 193
4 rue de la Bûcherie . 75005
01 43 54 08 24
galerieurubamba.com

**GALLERY S. BENSIMON** . . 45
111 rue de Turenne . 75003
01 42 74 50 77
gallerybensimon.com

**LE GARDE ROBE** . . . . . . . 23
41 rue de l'Arbre Sec . 75001
01 49 26 90 60

**GLASS** . . . . . . . . . . . . . . . 23
7 rue Frochot . 75009
09 80 72 98 83
glassparis.com

**LA GRANDE ÉPICERIE
DE PARIS** . . . . . . . . . . . . . 85
38 rue de Sèvres . 75007
01 44 39 81 00
lagrandeepicerie.com

# H

**HELMUT NEWCAKE** . . . . . 20
36 rue Bichat . 75010
09 82 59 00 39
helmutnewcake.com

**HERMÈS** . . . . . . . . . . . . . 85
17 rue de Sèvres . 75006
01 42 22 80 83
hermes.com

**HERVÉ CHÂTELAIN** . . . . . 77
140 rue Montmartre . 75002
01 45 08 85 57

**HOLYBELLY** . . . . . . . . . . . 25
19 rue Lucien Sampaix . 75010
09 73 60 13 64 . holybel.ly

**HOME AUTOUR DU MONDE** .45
12 rue des Francs Bourgeois
75003 . 01 42 77 16 18
bensimon.com

**HÔTEL DE NELL** . . . . . . . . 17
7–9 rue du Conservatoire . 75009
01 44 83 83 60
hoteldenell.com

**HÔTEL DU TEMPS** . . . . . . . 17
11 rue de Montholon . 75009
01 47 70 37 16
hotel-du-temps.fr

**HÔTEL JULES ET JIM** . . . . 17
11 rue des Gravilliers . 75003
01 44 54 13 13
hoteljulesetjim.com

**HÔTEL PARADIS** . . . . . . . . 17
41 rue des Petites écuries . 75010
01 45 23 08 22
hotelparadisparis.com

**L'HÔTEL PARTICULIER** . . . 75
23 avenue Junot, Pavillon D
75018 . 01 53 41 81 40
hotel-particulier-montmartre.com

# J-I

**IMPOSSIBLE** . . . . . . . . . . . 231
77 rue Charlot . 75003
09 54 18 67 82
shop.the-impossible-projet.com

**INDIA MAHDAVI** . . . . . . . . 49
3 & 19 rue Las cases . 75007
01 45 55 67 67
india-mahdavi.com

**ISAAC REINA** . . . . . . . . . . 236
38 rue de Sévigné . 75003
01 42 78 81 95 . isaac-reina.com

**IZAKAYA ISSÉ** . . . . . . . . . 76
45 rue de Richelieu . 75001
01 42 96 26 60

**IZRAËL** . . . . . . . . . . . . . . . 40
30 rue François Miron . 75004
01 42 72 66 23

JAMINI . . . . . . . . . . . . . . 187
10 rue du Châteaux d'Eau . 75010
09 82 34 78 53
jaminidesign.com

JARDIN DES PLANTES . . . 74
57 rue Cuvier . 75005

JARDIN DES TUILERIES . . 74
Place de la Concorde . 75001
01 44 50 75 01

JARDIN DES TUILERIES
BOOKSTORE . . . . . . . . . . . 74
Place de la Concorde . 75001
01 42 60 61 61

JARDIN
DU LUXEMBOURG. . . . . . . 74
Corner of rue de Médicis
& rueVaugirard . 75006

JARDIN DU MUSÉE
CARNAVALET . . . . . . . . . . 74
23 rue de Sévigné . 75003
01 44 59 58 58

JARDIN SAINT-GILLES-
GRAND-VENEUR . . . . . . . . 74
12 rue Villehardouin . 75003

JEAN-MARC POURSIN . . . 35
35 rue des Vinaigriers . 75010

JEAN-PAUL HÉVIN . . . . . . 20
231 rue Saint-Honoré . 75001
01 55 35 35 96
jeanpaulhevin.com

JÉRÔME LEPERT. . . . . . . .151
106 rue Vieille du Temple
75003
06 10 18 18 88

JOURNAL STANDARD
DE LUXE . . . . . . . . . . . . . .226
11–12 galerie de Montpensier
75001 . journal-standard.jp

K

KANN DESIGN . . . . . . . . . . 35
28 rue des Vinaigriers . 75010
09 53 40 86 98
kanndesign.com

KB . . . . . . . . . . . . . . . . . . . . 25
62 rue des Martyrs . 75009
01 56 92 12 41

KHADI AND CO . . . . . . . . 235
37 rue Debelleyme . 75003
khadiandco.com

KIDIMO. . . . . . . . . . . . . . . 150
227 rue Saint-Denis . 75002
kidimo.com

KILIM ADA . . . . . . . . . . . . 61
52 rue des Archives . 75004
01 42 78 03 02
34 rue des Écoles . 75005
01 43 29 54 77 kilims.fr

KILIWATCH. . . . . . . . . . . .229
64 rue Tiquetonne . 75002
01 42 21 17 37
espacekiliwatch.fr

KUNITORAYA. . . . . . . . . . . 19
1 rue Villedo . 75001
01 47 03 33 65 . kunitoraya.com

L

LADURÉE . . . . . . . . . . . . . 21
16–18 rue Royale . 75008
01 42 60 21 79

LAURETTE . . . . . . . . . . . . 251
18 rue Mabillon . 75006
01 46 34 35 22
laurette-deco.com

LAVERDURE & FILS. . . . . 106
58 rue Traversière . 75012
01 43 43 38 85 laverdure.fr

LAVRUT . . . . . . . . . . . . . 102
52 passage Choiseul . 75002
01 42 96 95 54
adam-lavrut.com

LEGERON. . . . . . . . . . . . . 109
20 rue des Petits Champs . 75002
01 42 96 94 89 . legeron.com

LIBRAIRIE
ALAIN BRIEUX. . . . . . . . . 168
48 rue Jacob . 75006
01 42 60 21 98 . alainbrieux.com

LIBRAIRIE ELBÉ . . . . . . . 169
213 bd Saint-Germain . 75007
01 45 48 77 97

LINDELL AND CO . . . . . . 63
14 rue du Grand Prieuré . 75011
01 43 57 43 42
lindellandco.com

THE LITTLE RED DOOR . . 23
60 rue Charlot . 75003
01 42 71 19 32
lrdparis.com

THE LITTLE SHOP
OF COLOURS. . . . . . . . . . 129
1 rue de Jarente . 75004
01 42 71 36 75
tlsparis.com

LOFT DESIGN BY. . . . . . . 35
29 rue des Vinaigriers . 75010
09 80 94 55 59
loftdesignby.com

LE LOIR DANS
LA THÉIÈRE . . . . . . . . . . . 20
3 rue des Rosiers . 75004
01 42 72 90 61

LE LOUSTIC . . . . . . . . . . . 25
40 rue Chapon . 75003
09 80 31 07 06

LUDOVIC MESSAGER . . . 174
Puces de St-Ouen, 3 Rue Paul Bert
06 18 99 18 25

M

MAHATSARA . . . . . . . . . . 196
8 rue Oberkampf . 75011
01 58 30 89 29
mahatsara.com

MAISON & OBJET . . . . . . . . 6
93420 Villepinte

LA MAISON DE
LA PORCELAINE . . . . . . . 216
21 rue de Paradis . 75010
01 47 70 22 80
maisonporcelaine.com

LA MAISON
DU CHOCOLAT . . . . . . . . 21
8 bd de la Madeleine . 75009
01 47 42 86 52
lamaisonduchocolat.com

LA MAISON DU PASTEL . . 99
20 rue Rambuteau . 75003
01 40 29 00 67
lamaisondupastel.com

MAISON M . . . . . . . . . . . . . 43
25 rue de Bourgogne . 75007
01 47 53 07 74
maisonmparis.com

**MAMIE GÂTEAUX** . . . . . . **250**
66 rue du Cherche-Midi . 75006
01 42 22 32 15
mamie-gateaux.com

**MANDORLA PALACE** . . . **244**
34 rue François Miron . 75004
01 48 04 71 24
mandorlapalace.canalblog.com

**LA MANUFACTURE
ALAIN DUCASSE** . . . . . . . . **21**
40 rue de la Roquette . 75011
01 48 05 82 86
lechocolat-alainducasse.com

**MARCEL BY** . . . . . . . . . . . **41**
28 rue Saint-Claude . 75003
01 57 40 80 77
marcelby.fr

**MARCHÉ AUX FLEURS
ET AUX OISEAUX** . . . . . . . **93**
Place Louis Lépine & quai de la
Corse . 75004

**MARCHÉ BIOLOGIQUE
DES BATIGNOLLES** . . . . . . **26**
34 boulevard des Batignolles
75017

**MARCHÉ COUVERT
DES ENFANTS ROUGES** . . **26**
39 rue de Bretagne . 75003

**MARCHÉ D'ALIGRE** . . . . . . **26**
Place d'Aligre . 75012

**MARCHÉ D'ANVERS** . . . . . **26**
Place d'Anvers . 75009

**MARCHÉ DE LA PLACE
DES FÊTES** . . . . . . . . . . . . **26**
Place des Fêtes . 75019

**MARCHÉ DU
PRÉSIDENT WILSON** . . . . **26**
Avenue du Président Wilson
75016

**LE MARCHÉ RASPAIL** . . . . **27**
Boulevard Raspail . 75006

**MARCHÉ SAINT-PIERRE** . . **69**
2 rue Charles Nodier . 75018

**MARION HELD JAVAL** . . . **162**
21 rue de l'Odéon . 75006
01 43 29 96 91

**MARION VIDAL** . . . . . . . . **237**
13 avenue Trudaine . 75009
01 49 24 04 01
marionvidal.com

**LE MARY CÉLESTE** . . . . . . **47**
1 rue Commines . 75003
lemaryceleste.com

**MATHIAS ROUDINE** . . . . . . **181**
Puces de St-Ouen, Marché Paul Bert
96 rue des Rosiers
Allée 5, Stand 247
06 20 63 06 94

**LES MAUVAISES
GRAINES** . . . . . . . . . . . . . **80**
25 rue Custine . 75018
01 55 79 71 35
lesmauvaisesgraines.com

**MERCADIER** . . . . . . . . . . **133**
16 passage du Chantier . 75012
01 49 28 97 53
paris.mercadier.fr

**MERCI** . . . . . . . . . . . . . . . **203**
111 bd Beaumarchais . 75003
01 42 77 00 33
merci-merci.com

**MERVEILLEUX** . . . . . . . . . **21**
94 rue Saint-Dominique . 75007
01 47 53 91 34
auxmerveilleux.com

**MILLIMÈTRES** . . . . . . . . . **253**
19 rue Milton
75009 . 01 71 70 96 99
millimetres.fr

**MILLER ET BERTAUX** . . . . **87**
17 rue Ferdinand Duval . 75004
01 42 78 28 39
milleretbertaux.com

**MISE EN TEINTE** . . . . . . . **130**
15 bd Saint-Germain . 75005
01 46 34 44 58
miseenteinte.com

**MOKUBA** . . . . . . . . . . . . . **232**
18 rue Montmartre . 75001
01 40 13 81 41
mokuba.fr

**MON VIEIL AMI** . . . . . . . . . **13**
69 rue Saint-Louis-en-l'Île . 75004
01 40 46 01 35
mon-vieil-ami.com

**MONA MARKET** . . . . . . . . **47**
4 rue Commines . 75003
01 42 78 80 04
monamarket.com

**MORA** . . . . . . . . . . . . . . . **207**
13 rue Montmartre . 75001
01 45 08 19 24 . mora.fr

**MUSÉE DE LA VIE
ROMANTIQUE** . . . . . . . . . . **75**
16 rue Chaptal . 75009
01 55 31 95 67

**MUSKHANE** . . . . . . . . . . . **245**
3 rue Pastourelle . 75003
09 77 06 53 47
muskhane.fr

# N-O

**NO FACTORY** . . . . . . . . . . **145**
2 rue de l'Hôpital Saint-Louis
75010 . 06 09 64 75 99
nofactory.fr

**OBJET CÉLESTE** . . . . . . . **145**
34 bis rue Bichat . 75010
01 53 19 04 64

**ODEUR DE SAINTETÉ** . . . . **86**
22 quai du Louvre . 75001
01 42 21 38 33 (by app't)
odeurdesaintete.com

**ODORANTES** . . . . . . . . . . **78**
9 rue Madame . 75006
01 42 84 03 00
odorantes-paris.com

**L'OEIL DU PÉLICAN** . . . . **152**
13 rue Jean-Jacques Rousseau
75001
01 40 13 70 00
loeildupelican.fr

**OUMA PRODUCTIONS** . . **197**
8 impasse Saint-Sébastien
75011
06 14 31 32 48

# P

**PAIN DE SUCRE** . . . . . . . . **99**
14 rue Rambuteau . 75004
01 45 74 68 92
patisseriepaindesucre.com

**PAIN D'ÉPICES** . . . . . . . . **247**
29 passage Jouffroy . 75009
01 47 70 08 68
paindepices.fr

**PAPIER PLUS** . . . . . . . . . **101**
9 rue du Pont Louis-Philippe
75004 . 01 42 77 70 49
papierplus.com

**PAPIER TIGRE** . . . . . . . . . 43
5 rue des Filles du calvaire
75003 . 01 48 04 00 21
papiertigre.fr

**PARC DE SCEAUX** . . . . . . . 74
92330 Sceaux

**PÂTISSERIE CIEL** . . . . . . . . 21
3 rue Monge . 75005
01 43 29 40 78
patisserie-ciel.com

**LA PÂTISSERIE
CYRIL LIGNAC** . . . . . . . . . 124
24 rue Paul Bert . 75011
01 43 72 74 88

**PATRICIA VIELJEUX** . . . . . 112
21 rue Godefroy Cavaignac
75011 . 01 46 59 04 10
patriciavieljeux.com

**PEAUSSERIE POULAIN** . . . 111
52 bd Richard Lenoir . 75011
01 48 05 54 54
peausseriepoulain.com

**LES PEINTURES XVIIIe** . . . 80
34 rue Custine . 75018
01 42 51 05 07
paint-papers.com

**PEP'S** . . . . . . . . . . . . . . 150
223 rue Saint-Martin
passage de l'Ancre . 75003
01 42 78 11 67
peps-paris.com

**PEPA'S** . . . . . . . . . . . . . 251
40 rue des Petits carreaux
75002 . 01 42 36 06 77
pepaskids.com

**LE PERCHOIR** . . . . . . . . 190
14 rue Crespin du gast . 75011
01 48 06 18 48

**PERIGOT** . . . . . . . . . . . . 211
16 bd des Capucines . 75009
01 53 40 98 90 . perigot.fr

**PERSONA GRATA** . . . . . . 46
71 bd de Sébastopol . 75002
01 42 33 15 15
persona-grata.com

**LE PETIT FABLAB** . . . . . . 123
156 rue Oberkampf . 75011

**LA PETITE MAISON** . . . . . 176
Puces de St-Ouen, Marché Paul Bert
6 rue Paul Bert
01 40 10 56 69

**PETIT PAN** . . . . . . . . . . . 244
37, 39 & 76 rue François Miron
75004 . 09 80 44 85 51
95 rue du Bac . 75007
01 45 48 72 25
10 rue Yvonnes Le Tac . 75018
01 42 23 63 78
petitpan.com

**PHONOGALERIE** . . . . . . . 159
10 rue Lallier . 75009
01 45 26 45 80 . phonogalerie.com

**PIERRE & VESTIGES** . . . . 135
26 rue Henri Régnault
92150 Suresnes
01 45 06 26 94 . andree-mace.com

**PIERRE HERMÉ** . . . . . . . . 21
72 rue Bonaparte . 75006
01 43 54 47 77 . pierreherme.com

**LA PIÑATA** . . . . . . . . . . . 35
25 rue des Vinaigriers . 75010
01 40 35 01 45 . lapinata.fr

**POPELINI** . . . . . . . . . . . . 21
29 rue Debelleyme . 75003
01 44 61 31 44
44 rue des Martyrs . 75009
01 42 81 35 79 . popelini.com

**PORTOBELLO** . . . . . . . . . 36
32 rue du Roi de Sicile . 75004
01 42 72 27 74
portobello-decoration.fr

**POUR VOS
BEAUX YEUX** . . . . . . . . . 227
10 passage du Grand-Cerf . 75002
01 42 36 06 79
pourvosbeauxyeux.com

**PUCES DE SAINT-OUEN** . . 171
93400 Saint Ouen

**PUCES DE VANVES** . . . . . 138
Avenue Georges Lafenestre
75014

**LE PURE CAFÉ** . . . . . . . . 124
14 rue Jean Macé . 75011
01 43 71 47 22 . purecafe.fr

**RACINES** . . . . . . . . . . . . . 77
8 passage des Panoramas
75002 . 01 40 13 06 41

**RALPH LAUREN
VINTAGE** . . . . . . . . . . . . . 229
173 bd Saint-Germain . 75006
01 44 77 76 00
ralphlaurenstgermain.com/fr

**RD SPECTACLES** . . . . . . . 109
82 rue de Cléry . 75002
01 40 26 71 86 . rd-spectacles.fr

**LA RÉGALADE
SAINT-HONORÉ** . . . . . . . . 13
123 rue Saint-Honoré . 75001
01 42 21 92 40

**RESSOURCE** . . . . . . . . . . 132
62 rue la Boétie . 75008
01 45 61 38 05
2–4 avenue du Maine . 75015
01 42 22 58 80
ressource-peintures.com

**LE RICHER** . . . . . . . . . . . 19
2 rue Richer . 75010

**RICKSHAW** . . . . . . . . . . . 192
7 passage du Grand-Cerf
75002 . 01 42 21 41 03
rickshaw.fr

**LE ROSA BONHEUR** . . . . . 23
2 avenue des Cascades . 75019
01 42 00 00 45 . rosabonheur.fr

**RUE HEROLD** . . . . . . . . . . 59
8 rue Herold . 75001
01 42 33 66 56 . rueherold.fr

**SACHA FINKELSZTAJN** . . 87
27 rue des Rosiers . 75004
01 42 72 78 91
finkelsztajn.com

**SACRÉS COUPONS** . . . . . 69
4 bis rue d'Orsel . 75018
01 42 64 69 96

**SARAH LAVOINE** . . . . . . . 34
9 rue Saint-Roch . 75001
01 42 96 34 35
28 rue du Bac . 75007
01 42 86 00 35
sarahlavoine.com

**SÉBASTIEN GAUDARD** . . . 20
22 rue des Martyrs . 75009
01 71 18 24 70
sebastiengaudard.com

**SECRET MAISON** . . . . . . . . 91
17 rue des Quatre Vents . 75006
01 42 05 09 09 . secretmaison.fr

**SENNELIER – LES COULEURS
DU QUAI** . . . . . . . . . . . . . 104
3 quai Voltaire . 75007
01 42 60 72 15
magasinsennelier.com

**SEPTIME** . . . . . . . . . . . . . . 19
80 rue de Charonne . 75011
01 43 67 38 29
septime-charonne.fr

**SERENDIPITY** . . . . . . . . . . 250
81 rue du Cherche-Midi . 75006
01 40 46 01 15 . serendipity.fr

**LE SERGENT RECRUTEUR** . 19
41 rue Saint-Louis-en-l'Île . 75004
01 43 54 75 42
lesergentrecruteur.fr

**SHANGRI-LA HOTEL BAR** . . 23
10 avenue d'Iena . 75016
01 53 67 19 98
shangri-la.com/paris

**SHINDO** . . . . . . . . . . . . . 233
2 rue d'Aboukir . 75002
01 44 88 27 57 . shindo.fr

**UN SINGE EN HIVER** . . . . 175
Puces de St-Ouen, Marché Paul Bert
6 rue Paul Bert . 06 75 55 44 57
unsingeenhiver.com

**LA SOIE DISANTE** . . . . . . . 67
36 rue de Verneuil . 75007
01 42 61 23 44

**SOL SEMILLA** . . . . . . . . . . 35
23 rue des Vinaigriers . 75010
01 42 01 03 44 . sol-semilla.fr

**STÉPHANE CHAPELLE** . . . 76
29 rue de Richelieu . 75001
01 42 60 65 66

**TALENTS** . . . . . . . . . . . . . .115
1bis rue Scribe . 75009
01 40 17 98 38

**TARTAIX** . . . . . . . . . . . . . .121
13-15 rue du Pont-aux-Choux
75003 . 01 42 72 02 63
tartaix.com

**TÉLESCOPE** . . . . . . . . . . . 25
5 rue Villedo . 75001
01 42 61 33 14
telescopecafe.com

**TEN BELLES** . . . . . . . . . . . 25
10 rue de la Grange aux Belles
75010 . 01 42 40 90 78
tenbelles.com

**TERROIRS D'AVENIR** . . . . . 27
6-7-8 rue du Nil . 75002
01 45 08 48 80

**TISSUS REINE** . . . . . . . . . 69
3–5 place Saint-Pierre . 75018
01 46 06 02 31
tissus-reine.com

**TOMBÉES DU CAMION** . . 147
17 rue Joseph de Maistre
75018
09 81 21 62 80
tombeesducamion.com

**LA TRÉSORERIE** . . . . . . . 219
11 rue du Châteaux d'Eau
75010
01 40 40 20 46
latresorerie.fr

**TSÉ & TSÉ** . . . . . . . . . . . 213
7 rue Saint-Roch . 75001
01 42 61 90 26
tse-tse.com

**TUCK SHOP** . . . . . . . . . . . 25
13 rue Lucien Sampaix
75010 . 09 80 72 95 40

**ULTRAMOD** . . . . . . . . . . 224
3–4 rue de Choiseul . 75002
01 42 96 98 30

**UNTITLED** . . . . . . . . . . . . 178
Puces de St-Ouen, Marché Paul Bert
96 rue des Rosiers
Allée 1, Stand 122
untitled-clothes.fr

**UP** . . . . . . . . . . . . . . . . . 210
14 rue Froissard . 75003

**VERJUS** . . . . . . . . . . . . . . 23
52 rue de Richelieu . 75001
01 42 97 54 40
verjusparis.com

**LA VERRERIE
DES HALLES** . . . . . . . . . .205
15 rue du Louvre . 75001
01 42 36 86 02
verrerie-des-halles-paris.fr

**VILMORIN** . . . . . . . . . . . . . 93
6 quai de la Mégisserie . 75001
01 42 33 61 62
vilmorin-jardin.fr

**VINCENT GUERRE** . . . . . . 136
20 rue Chauchat . 75009
01 42 46 48 50

**WEBER** . . . . . . . . . . . . . . 123
9 rue de Poitou / 66 rue de Turenne
75003 . 01 46 72 34 00
weber-metaux.com

**XANADOU** . . . . . . . . . . . . 210
10 rue Saint-Sulpice . 75006
01 43 26 73 43

**YVELINE** . . . . . . . . . . . . . . 163
4 rue de Furstemberg . 75006
01 43 26 56 91
yveline-antiquites.com

**YVES ANDRIEUX
& VINCENT JALBERT** . . . 231
55 rue Charlot . 75003
01 42 71 19 54
vincentjalbert.com

**ZERO ONE ONE** . . . . . . . . 210
2 rue de Marengo . 75001
01 49 27 00 11
zerooneone.blogspot.com

**ZUT!** . . . . . . . . . . . . . . . . 144
9 rue Ravignan . 75018
01 42 59 69 68
antiquites-industrielles.com

Published in 2015 by Murdoch Books, an imprint of Allen & Unwin
First published by Hachette Livre (Marabout) in 2014

Murdoch Books Australia
83 Alexander Street
Crows Nest NSW 2065
Phone: +61 (0) 2 8425 0100
www.murdochbooks.com.au
info@murdochbooks.com.au

Murdoch Books UK
Erico House, 6th Floor
93–99 Upper Richmond Road
Putney, London SW15 2TG
Phone: +44 (0) 20 8785 5995
www.murdochbooks.co.uk
info@murdochbooks.co.uk

For Corporate Orders & Custom Publishing contact Noel Hammond,
National Business Development Manager, Murdoch Books Australia

Publisher: Corinne Roberts
Text and photographs: Elodie Rambaud
(except photograph page 18 top © Benoist Linero)
Layout: Fabien Barral
Translator: Melissa McMahon
Editor: Shan Wolody
Designer: Katy Wall
Production manager: Mary Bjelobrk

Text and Design © Hachette Livre (Marabout) 2014

A cataloguing-in-publication entry is available from the catalogue of the National Library
of Australia at nla.gov.au.

ISBN 978 1 74336 464 2 Australia
ISBN 978 1 74336 465 9 UK

A catalogue record for this book is available from the British Library.

Colour reproduction by Splitting Image, Clayton, Victoria

Printed by 1010 Printing International Limited, China